Just Buy Her a Dress and She'll Be Fine

A true story about Postpartum OCD, Anxiety, and Depression; about losing yourself, losing your spouse, losing your religion, losing your mind and finding them all again

1

This book can be purchased in paperback or Kindle form at Amazon.com or if you go to https://smile.amazon.com/ to purchase and select "Postpartum Support International" as your charity, Amazon will donate 0.5% of your purchase to them or another charity you choose.

Please also follow and like the Facebook page to keep up with the Author and for funny, inspirational and informative posts about postpartum mood disorders and parenting.

fb.me/JustBuyHeraDress

* The author will donate at least 10% of the proceeds of this book to various charities and organizations in order to provide support for, and raise even more awareness of Postpartum OCD, Anxiety, Depression and other postpartum mood disorders.

"The moment a child is born, the mother is also born. She never existed before. The woman existed, but the mother; never. A mother is something absolutely new." ~Rajneesh

Dedicated to my baby girl, Aubrie Lynn. You will always be my baby girl. Most parents call their children sweet. Some days we call you sweet, but more often we joke you are as mean as a hornet or a snake. However, we do call you beautiful, smart, funny, social, tough, and stubborn and would say you have more personality than any other child we have ever seen. You have taught me and your Daddy more about life, ourselves and each other than anyone else ever has and you continue to every day. We love you so much!

Acknowledgment

*Thanks to my husband Jay. We have been through a lot in the last 20 plus years, but I have had the best times of my life with you. I have also experienced the worst, but if it weren't for those, I wouldn't have been able to write this book. Just like you, I hope we look back together at 90 and laugh at how naive we were in our 20's. I love you!

*Thanks to my mom and stepdad for always making me feel worthy of love, which coincidentally is what my name "Amanda" means. You gave me self-confidence and made me feel I can accomplish anything.

*Thanks to my siblings, who are not only my friends but taught me more than you realize. Even when you were getting into trouble, I was learning from it too.

*Thanks to my friend Dorie for inviting me back to church, and to my Sunday school class who gave me unconditional love and support when I needed it most.

*Thanks to my friend Chrissy for encouraging me to give more people goosebumps and epiphanies.

 *Thanks to my co-workers, past and present, for getting me through work each day during the hardest time of my life.

* Thanks to Dr. Aizenman and Dr. Lott for their role in getting me better mentally and physically and for truly

listening and caring. Thanks to Dr. Ross for helping deliver my beautiful baby girl and my beautiful nieces.

*Thanks to all of you who were always there when I needed you, no matter what. Thank you for listening when I needed it most and for checking on me, no matter how far away you were.

*Thanks to all of you who shared your own stories with me and for reminding me that I was not alone.

*In memory of my father, William Earl Dodson, Jr. who lost his own battle with mental illness and addiction in 2007.

Preface

Right after I found out I was pregnant, my real
father passed away. I hadn't spoken to him or his side of
the family in three years. I was raised by my stepdad and
he was giving me away on my invitations and in my
wedding. My dad and his family were not happy about it.
I didn't go to my dad's funeral because I was afraid that I
might get so upset I would lose the baby. That was not the
least stressful way to start my pregnancy.

My pregnancy was planned because I am a planner,
or I was a planner. After all I have been through, I don't
plan much now. My husband and I both really wanted a
baby and had no trouble getting pregnant. I think we both
expected parenting to be easy. We had both taken care of
kids a lot before and loved children. We thought that we
would be wonderful parents. These expectations are
another thing that I think would later cause some issues for
me and probably contributed somewhat to my Anxiety and
Obsessive-Compulsive Disorder (OCD) getting so bad
postpartum.

Looking back now, I can see signs of Postpartum
OCD/Anxiety/Depression when I first had my daughter. I
had a great experience giving birth and Aubrie was healthy.
Although it was very painful, I chose to try to have her with
no epidural and was successful. When you do this, your
body releases natural drugs so I felt on a high for about 48
hours afterwards and felt great!

I wouldn't say that I didn't feel bonded to my baby
and really had no obvious signs in the hospital that
anything was wrong. However, as soon as we got home the
soreness began to kick in and the hormones must have
affected me, too. I started crying for no reason. I even

laughed while crying and told my husband that I knew I was crying because of hormones but I couldn't stop. He told me to go lie down because I needed the rest more. He had taken off two weeks to stay home and help. I chalked it up to having "baby blues" as I had heard that 80% of women get that and later, I seemed fine.

Even doing the littlest things that I had done so many times with other babies before now seemed so hard. Of course, I was sleep deprived for the first time in my life. I was one of those people who usually slept through the night without even getting up once for nine hours straight. Towards the end of my pregnancy, I got a little practice to prepare myself for the sleep deprivation because of discomfort and constantly having to use the bathroom. My husband and I were a pretty good parenting team at first, so I made it through the constant getting up during the night just fine, even once I went back to work.

I had been at the same job for a while, so I was able to take the whole twelve weeks of maternity leave. Aubrie was born right around the time that the weather was getting warm. We went out a lot and she didn't even get sick at all until winter came. Even then it was just a cold. She was and still is a very healthy child. I really enjoyed my maternity leave with her, but things started to get hard later in the year.

About seven months after I had Aubrie, my grandfather passed away. Then a little over a month later, I was laid off from my job. Even though I ended up with a good job six months later, I had an awful temp job in between and there was a lot of time when I had no work at all. I had a lot of interviews while also staying home with Aubrie, so I felt as if I had two jobs. When I started my new job, I was making less money and I had to work a lot of hours at first. All this really started to affect me. Looking back, my family can see a change in me around that time. My husband started working even more, and whether subconsciously or not, this was probably because he did not want to be around me as much.

I have always joked about being OCD, but it got so bad during this time and after that I cared more about the housework and yard work being done than I did about spending time with my family. I would say that I regretted having Aubrie and I would get jealous of her, which would hurt my husband. I even told him at one point that there were nights that I had gone to bed praying that I wouldn't wake up. I told him that for the first time in my life, I questioned if God even existed.

By the time I was really saying stuff like that out loud to him, he was so affected by everything himself that he wasn't thinking clearly either. The compulsive cleaning lunatic who was jealous of our daughter and wanted to die was not his wife, and this man was not my husband. I was too ashamed of my thoughts to tell anyone other than him. He had also never been very religious like me, so he had no idea how devastating losing my faith was for me.

Shortly after Aubrie turned two, my husband left, and he thought that he wanted a divorce. When he left, I lost it. That was when I finally got so bad that everyone realized something was wrong with me and I got help. I took one day off work. After that, I still went to work and took care of our daughter every day. Most days I just wanted to lie in bed or give up and be committed somewhere. I was so worn out. I couldn't sleep at night. Instead I would write out everything that I was thinking as I looked back over the last year or two to figure out went wrong. As I did this, it helped me start to figure things out.

I told my doctor that I thought I had Postpartum Depression. He had thought I had Obsessive Compulsive Disorder and Anxiety caused by the OCD for years and tried to get me on medication before. Much later I would realize he was right. When you do have them before having a child, it can get severe postpartum due to hormones and/or environmental factors such as the loss of a job and/or loss of loved ones, etc. All I knew at the time was my OCD and Anxiety were extremely higher than usual and majorly affecting my life. I also knew that not wanting to live anymore and wanting to run away sometimes were Postpartum Depression symptoms and I had experienced both. I had never even heard of Postpartum OCD or Postpartum Anxiety.

Depression, Anxiety, OCD, Postpartum Depression, Postpartum Anxiety, Postpartum OCD and Post-Traumatic Stress Disorder all have similar symptoms and treatment options.   In my quest to get better, I researched all of them. I had already researched some of them before this, along with bipolar disorder because I helped diagnose a family member with it. There is a history of mental illness on both sides of my family. At the doctor, when they ask you to fill out that form about your family's medical history, when I get to mental illness I just write, "multiple people, both sides". I joke about this all the time, even though it is true.

I think that most of them with it in the last two generations went undiagnosed because of the lack of knowledge about it at the time. I feel like their lives might have been completely different had they gotten the help they needed or if everyone around them had even just understood what they were struggling with. One of those people was my father, which is why this book is in memory of him. I am not a doctor or a professional in this area, although some jokingly called me Dr. Amanda during all of this because I seemed to think I knew it all. Everything in this book is based on my own experience and research that I did, which was apparently enough to fill a book. Any advice I give in the book does start with talking to an actual doctor.

After Jay left, Aubrie and I stayed with my mom and stepdad for about three months. After going to the doctor and getting on medication, my husband and I went to therapy. I also started going to church again. I began exercising and taking better care of myself and working less. I made up with my Dad's side of the family. I made more time for myself, my husband, and my friends and I spent less time doing chores, planning and obsessing over perfection. After being on again and off again for a year and a half, my husband finally moved back home for good. Aubrie and I were both doing very well. You could see a great change in her behavior as I got better. Things were starting to be like I had always thought they would be before I had Aubrie.

While I was recovering, I put some things on Facebook and sent emails that I shouldn't have. My sense of embarrassment and filter were almost completely gone. However, some good did come from this. I started writing blogs on Facebook about my experience. Upon reading these posts, people started sending me confidential messages about going through similar situations. Some were people I knew well; some I barely knew. People even started sharing stories with me in person, even people in my own family. Talking to other people who had been in similar situations helped me more than anything else and it also seemed to help them. That is what inspired me to write this book.

I have wanted to write a book since I was a child and finally had something to write about. I want to help and educate others. Most I know had not heard of Postpartum OCD or Anxiety. I checked to see how many books were already written and could not find many on Postpartum OCD. I also could not find many books on mood disorders with humor in them. I found many books on Postpartum Anxiety and a ton more on Postpartum Depression, yet people still have a lot of misconceptions about those as well. When people think of postpartum mood disorders, I want people to see their mom, their wife, their sister, their daughter as the people who could or have had them. Currently I feel so many people still think about someone like Andrea Yates.

Most stories like this on the news are Postpartum Psychosis not Postpartum Depression, Anxiety or OCD. It is much less common and most women with it still do not harm themselves or their child. These stories should still inspire people to try and prevent others from getting to that point or to get help themselves, but stories like this being what comes to people's minds also makes others scared to ask for help or speak up. They fear their children being taken away.

Table of Contents

Chapter 11: Can I have a Do-Over Please?

Chapter 1

I was Born Just Plain White Trash but Fancy Wasn't My Name

My mom did not like the name of this chapter when she first saw it. For one thing, she didn't know the Reba McEntire song I was referencing. Also, just like when my sister first saw the original title of the book and had the same reaction, she didn't understand I was trying to make light of something serious, which I do throughout this entire book. The reason I do that is, finally being able to laugh about it was the beginning of true recovery for me. When I first wrote this book, it was the name of another Chapter in here, *This Isn't the Kid I Ordered*. Some people took this the wrong way. One friend even said Aubrie would hate me one day for writing a book named that. The name was about parenting and my child not being like I expected, but in a good way. It was about the fact that I was such a planner and so obsessive compulsive that I had a certain way life was supposed to go, and when it didn't, my life unraveled for a bit.

My daughter is eleven now, she understood the first title and did not take offense to it. She knows she is very loved and wanted, and knows I went through a lot when she was first born that had nothing to do with her. She also knows her dad and I went through a hard time and almost split up before she was too young to remember, but we worked it out. I plan to continue to talk to her about it more and more and educate her as she gets older, especially in case she ever goes through the same. She did like me changing the name to Just Buy Her and She will Fine though, because she understood how others could take the title in the wrong way. After thinking about it more, I really liked the new title better anyways. It focused more on how women are treated after childbirth and how that often results in or worsens postpartum mood disorders.

The picture of my daughter screaming in my lap on the back of the outside of this book, while I try to smile with dark circles in my eyes, is what I call the picture of my Postpartum OCD/Anxiety/Depression. You won't see this if you are reading the eBook, but it is also on the book's Facebook page. It was taken in the middle of a family reunion well before anyone realized anything was wrong with me. There are also many happy normal pictures during this time though too. I can see it more when I watch some videos during that time. One moment I am laughing and interacting for the camera and the next staring off in the distance like I am bored out of my mind or off in another world.

Getting back to the title of this chapter, many people I know have no idea that I lived in what most people would consider a shack until I was six years old. We lived in the country in Eastaboga, Alabama close to Anniston. Shortly after I turned six, we moved very close to the big city of Columbia, South Carolina. We lived in a small rented brick home. My mom paid a lady we knew to walk me and my sister to and from the school bus each day. My sister was only two years older than me and we had to get on it in a bad part of town. Despite this, I don't recall anything scary ever happening and I remember everyone on our bus being nice to us. Two years later we would end up moving back to the country in Alabama, into a little bit nicer rented brick home on three acres. This time we were moving to East Limestone, Alabama. It was close to Huntsville and only a couple hours from our family in Anniston.

We moved three times growing up but the last time we had finally made it to middle class. We moved only a couple hours away close to Birmingham to a town called Alabaster. This move was the hardest adjustment yet. We went from a school that had as many students in Kindergarten through Twelfth grade as they did in this new school in Ninth grade through Twelfth grade. Where we came from, I was friends with almost everyone my age. I was in sixth grade at the time. There were already cliques at this new school in sixth grade. I was eventually accepted into the goody-two-shoes clique mainly because that was the group that was nice to almost everyone and took me in and because, at the time, I was a goody-two-shoes.

Before we moved here my best friend was not a goody-two shoes, but we sort of balanced each other. She made sure I had plenty of fun and I made sure we didn't get into too much trouble. Who wants to hang out with people just like them? How boring, right? That is how it seemed to work here though. Looking back, I think I had depression when we moved. I cried all the time for almost two years, got migraine headaches and made excuses not to go to school.

Within a couple years, I grew comfortable in my group. I finally liked living in the new place and the year after growing comfortable I would end up meeting my future husband. Part of what bonded us was he went through the same thing. He had to move close to the same age. Moving did have its benefits other than just moving up to middle class. I was very shy as a child and was forced out of my shell. Going to Auburn and changing jobs a couple of times as an adult, along with being forced to speak, and even dance in front of others at school and work continued to bring me further out of my shell.

Regardless of what clique you were in almost every person in this new school seemed to be well off compared to how I lived in my younger days. Most ended up going to college for at least a year and had brand name everything. When we got into high school, the cliques changed around some. The closer we got to graduation they seemed to finally start almost disappearing because we knew they soon would not matter anymore. In college and after, I eventually became friends with almost everyone I wasn't friends with during high school thanks in part to myspace and Facebook. My husband and I even started having people from school over and it was people from different cliques.

I am not embarrassed by my lower-class background. I bring it up when I have the chance. I am proud that my mom and stepdad both worked very hard to move us from poverty to middle class by the time I was twelve. Both came from families that did not have a lot of money and neither had a college degree. They came from families where morals and hard work were taught. I was actually very happy as a child even when we had little. It took me a long time to adjust to the change from lower class to middle class.

Now I just appreciate having such a different perspective than just the life I have now. A lot of people do not have that, and I think it helps you gain more empathy. I love going to visit my family members that don't have as much because everyone seems so much more down to earth. No one is worried about what kind of car you drive or what clothes you are wearing. I do appreciate the opportunities I have had though, that my parents and a lot of my family did not at a younger age.

The reason I am bringing this part of my background up is when I got depressed, I started going back trying to figure out how I got to that point. I started analyzing everything in my life. When I did, I realized the fact that I changed classes when I was younger had a huge impact on my life and who I became. Because my parents didn't go to college, they encouraged us to go so things would not be as hard for us. I already knew I wanted to go to college when I was three years old. Almost everyone in middle class went to college because their parents wanted them to and it was expected of them. While in college, I was surrounded by many people whose parents were paying for their school, they didn't have to work and they either failed out or took seven or eight years to get a four-year degree. There were some people who were doing it all on their own with no help that I admired for it. Most accomplished a lot later in life.

My real father and his parents paid for half of my school and my mom and stepdad helped me pay for part of the rest and for my spending and living expenses. I also got some scholarships, student loans and worked part-time jobs to help some myself. I finished in only three years in order to save money and start making money faster. I wanted to get married to my high school sweetheart and was in a hurry to grow up. Later, I wished that I had enjoyed college for a little longer. College was one of the best times of my life because you have all that freedom without all the responsibility yet. I think the only point in life that might beat it is retirement.

When I was younger, my mom and stepdad's families talked about most things openly. Most people in middle class did not seem to talk as openly about certain things.. So, I tried not to but when Jay left, I just lost it and overshared with everyone. Keeping it in had done me no good so I took the opposite approach. I did leave some of it out of this book though. I wanted to publish enough to help others and as much as some things would make this book much juicer, I am not trying to include anything that would embarrass anyone. I was eventually very embarrassed once I realized how much I had shared with others. I even had dreams about being nude in public. After having this same dream a few times, I looked for a meaning. The main one I found was feeling overexposed, and I did. I also had a recurring dream during this time about being forced to go back to high school or college and when I looked up the meaning of it, one that made sense to me was that I was wanting to go back to a time in life when things seemed easier which was also true.

I didn't speak my mind much when I was younger. When I did people didn't seem to like it. They seemed to like it more when I just went along with everything, so I usually did. I think that is why when I finally did speak my mind one day with my dad's family, a little bit too much came out. The fact that they quit talking to me for a while made me think that if you speak your mind you get abandoned. When I went through my depression, I kept my thoughts from everyone at first but gradually started telling them more and more to my husband to get his reaction. When I didn't get the reaction I wanted, and he eventually abandoned me too, I again felt bad for telling someone else what I was thinking.

When everyone my age got out of college, they all thought they had to have a house and car as nice as their parents when they graduated so I had to as well. You don't come out of college making much more, or sometimes any more than you would have without the degree. In most cases you do make more over a lifetime, but you must work your way up. That is not how it is made to appear to us when we are in college. Every generation is so hard on the one before. My generation gets picked on for expecting instant gratification by the generation before us that gave us trophies for everything, the internet, cell phones, microwaves, on demand, and easy access to a lot of debt. I think this instant gratification society has helped to cause what I like to jokingly call the Mental Illness fad.

Chapter 2

The Mental Illness Fad

So many young adults you talk to these days are
either currently on or have been on some form of
antidepressants, Anxiety medication, or ADD or ADHD or
OCD medicine, just to name a few of the most common,
and a lot have been to therapy. Until I went through severe
Postpartum OCD, Anxiety and Depression, I had never
taken any pills like that or been to therapy despite having
some OCD and Anxiety issues even before that. As a kid I
would do things like count how many steps it would take to
get across a room, try to get across in a certain number or
steps, line things up perfectly and purposely step over
cracks. As I got older, I started to wonder more and more if
everyone did stuff like that. It took me forever to pull my
hair back because it had to have no lumps, unless I was
working out or hanging out around the house. I rarely wore
my hair back any other time.

I try not to throw away soap bottles or toothpaste
until I get every drop out of it. This may not seem OCD,
but it would seem OCD if you knew how much time I
wasted thinking about it in the shower, and planning using
certain ones in certain order to use them up faster. I
experience some sense of accomplishment when I finish
one and throw it away. I am not sure why except maybe for
not wasting anything. My husband is probably reading this
right now and realizing for the first time that I even do this.
Growing up I would visit some family members who would
have 10 deodorants, 15 lotions, etc. I was stumped that
they struggled with money but had so much of these things.

Maybe this caused me to try to be the opposite, I don't know.

I have known many who were OCD in and outside of my family. Two people I knew washed their hands repeatedly so much that their hands would become raw. I knew another who plucked out all her eyelashes. Another must have radio knobs and other knobs in certain positions even when the radio or TV etc. is off. Another is an organized hoarder obsessed with cleaning.

I love the show *Scrubs* and Michael J. Fox co-starred on a couple of episodes where he played a doctor with OCD. He had been to therapy which allowed him to still be an amazing doctor and surgeon that many looked up to. He still repeatedly washed his hands, turn light switches on and off and would enter and/or exit a room until he thought he had done so perfectly. He would go home to use the restroom and only after cleaning it repeatedly first. He also did not like shaking hands but could handle it for a short time now thanks to therapy. I have heard Howie Mandell is the same way which is why everyone fist bumps him on *Deal or No Deal*.

The main character on the show *Scrubs* was kind of jealous of Michael J. Fox's character and how much everyone loved him. Then he sees him in one of his worst moments. He is really struggling with his OCD and compulsively washing his hands and kind of has a breakdown in front of him. He sees of course that he is not superhuman and like everyone else, struggles with his own demons. I have never had any of those symptoms and am far from a germaphobe. I do love things are clean and neat try to keep some keepsakes. I often get rid of important things and later regret it though because if everything does not have a place it stresses me out.

I used to stress about any light bulb not changed, any repairs not done, or anything not hung in the house, etc. When I say stress, I mean think about them all constantly. There was a constant to do list in my head. On medicine this is much easier to ignore but I still think about it more than most normal people. All mental illness looks different in different people. There are similarities but people all cope in different ways so symptoms will often be different. People with OCD obsess over different things.

I have always been a worrier with a racing mind. When I was in college, I started using a planner because I had so much to do. This eventually got out of control. Years later I would write down everything I had to do or couldn't remember. My husband used to jokingly ask if I had "breathe" written in there. I would put things in a planner so I could quit thinking about them constantly, but then my list would get so long and overwhelming that it would give me anxiety. When I started working in HR, I had to keep a separate planner for work so now I had two.

While getting treated for my Postpartum OCD and Anxiety, I lost my personal planner. I thought maybe that wasn't coincidence, so I decided to try and live without it. I kept the work one but eventually got rid of it too and mainly use my Outlook Calendar now. I found my personal planner two weeks after losing it and threw it in the garbage. To this day I still struggle not to over plan. I sometimes start making to do lists but must stop myself from going overboard, but without Outlook how else would I remember my daughter is supposed to wear all green tomorrow for some Dr. Seuss dress up day?

Before getting treated, I was one of those people who thought that people relied on both pills and therapy too much. Now that I was on the other side of the current Mental Illness Fad, I found myself battling judgment from those on the side I used to be on. I was hesitant about taking pills or therapy until my doctor talked me into both.

He assured me that the pills would not change me and said they would not even fix me. They only help to treat the physical symptoms, which makes it easier to do what you need to do to get better. I needed them in the same way diabetic needs insulin. He told me that therapy would not fix me either. All the therapist can do is to help you figure out what is wrong then you still must fix it. He was right.

The pills helped stopped panic attacks I was having for one. At first, I thought something was wrong with my heart and even had it checked. If you have never had a panic attack usually your heart starts beating very fast, you have trouble breathing and feel like you might faint. At least that is how they felt to me and I have heard others describe them the same. They sometimes happened in the morning as I was getting ready, but they also happened a lot when I was working out, which is usually when I am most relaxed.

I never thought of them being panic attacks until I had one when I had to see my husband for the first time after he left me. He was dropping our daughter off at my work as I was leaving so he could go to work. I remember being upset that she had a wet diaper and he had forgotten to pack any. I was going to walk her around my work to see everyone. When I say upset I mean crazy upset. I remember calling his mom leaving her a voicemail about him doing that like it was the worst thing on Earth. The pills helped with this overreacting as well and helped me eventually stop apologizing all the time. That was another symptom. I would do something, then feel bad, then apologize but then do it again and apologize again and so on, or apologize even when no one thought I did anything wrong. This would frustrate friends and family, but I really felt like I could not control it.

They also helped me stop getting sick to my stomach all the time as a result of stress. I also got my energy back. It helped me to not have constant racing thoughts so I could control my thoughts more and not have so many negative ones. They helped me to focus more and to think more about things before I said them. It takes time for the pills to work and the longer you take them the more they help. Some people never make it past the first two weeks because it doesn't make them instantly better.

They also aren't happy pills that make you see through rose-colored goggles. If that were true most of the people around you would be a lot happier since so many people are on antidepressants. They also do not work for everyone and some must seek other treatment options. Some also must try many different kinds and dosages before they find the right one for them. If you stay on them long term you also sometimes must change the type or dosage as you become immune to some over time.

Antidepressants are like birth control pills. If you do not take them as directed, antidepressants will not work, and you will be at even more risk for negative side effects. You must wean on and off these pills carefully and take them as your doctor directs you to. If you miss one, you must take proper precautions just like you would if you missed a birth control pill. I accidentally missed one early on when I was weaning on and when my husband upset me over the phone, I told him, "I will just go jump off a bridge then". The truth is that as I drove over bridges you could drive off sometimes or by walls you could drive into alone, I am pretty sure the thought quickly crossed my mind at times when I was at my worst. That is probably where that comment stemmed from. I have since talked to other new mothers who had the same thoughts.

So why is there so much mental illness now? There are many theories out there. One even involves a lack of vitamins such as magnesium in the foods we eat now compared to years ago. Also, these same illnesses were often either not treated in the past or not treated correctly. However, some still think we live in a more stressful time as well, especially here in the United States. We are the only major country that does not have paid maternity and/or paternity leave. We are also one of the few without universal healthcare. Many others have free or cheaper college and day care as well and work less hours than we do and have more vacation. We worry about sending our kids to school or going anywhere because of mass shootings. All these things make life and parenting overwhelming for so many.

Everyone wants everything now and we live in a world of technology. You cannot escape work or other people. You can always be reached by phone or email. There is no escape from stress. It is constant. Kids are also majorly overprotected these days so being a parent is more stressful than ever. My daughter loves to play with other kids but if any of her friends can play, some of their parents watch them constantly. They will not even allow 10-year old kids to play in their own yard by themselves. Even though crime is lower than it was when we were younger, thanks to the internet, Amber Alerts and 24-hour news we know where every sex predator lives, and we know about every kidnapping.

I watched a 14-year-old comedian online the other day and he joked that when he leaves the house, he must carry a whistle and binder full of all the local registered sex offenders. The parents who raised us are often the first to now be paranoid about us leaving our own older children home alone, at ages we were not only home alone but babysitting younger children. A lot of the things our parents did as kids or even we did as kids are illegal now.

I was at my grandmother's not too long ago and was sitting outside with my cousins watching our kids play. My cousins started to get onto their kids for going down a very small grassy ditch in a box. I laughed and pointed to the top of the hill, which was a gravel road that we used to fly down on our bikes with no helmets or knee pads. Our grandmother also taught us how to steer a wagon down that hill. Surprisingly, not only did we survive, we never even went to the emergency room. I did have a cousin though, on the other side of the family, who was bike riding with a friend once. I believe her friend hit a pothole, flew off the bike and died of a head injury, because most did not wear helmets back then.

I am of course not against helmets and knee pads, car seats, seat belts, etc. but as usual I feel like there is some happy medium between how protective we are now and how carefree we used to be. I always joke that germaphobes will be the end of us. Didn't anyone watch War of the Worlds? All my friends who are germaphobes are sick all the time and so are their kids. I hate hand sanitizer, Lysol and Clorox. The smell of all three makes me sick and I only use them when necessary. Although I started working at a daycare recently so they are now a regular part of clean up at work. I usually just stuck with soap and water and the two second rule before. At almost 4 years old, my child had never been to the doctor for anything except immunizations.

I recently found out that my best friend had never taken her daughter to a play place. Our daughters are almost the same age. I was stunned because that is one of Aubrie's favorite things to do. I love to pick on my friend about her germaphobia. I joked for her to brace herself as I told her that sometimes Aubrie even plays in them without socks. I eventually talked her into going with us and her daughter had the time of her life! We started out at Chick-fil-A and then progressed to McDonald's. I was so proud of her. I do understand where her fear stems from. Her daughter has had seizures from high fevers before.

However, she let this fear consume her and take over her life in some ways and her daughter's.

I have conquered a lot of fears over the last ten years, including dancing in front of other people and public speaking as I mentioned before. I even went on a work trip alone and flew alone for the first time and loved it because I had tons of time to myself. That is something I have learned to treasure since having a child. I have also conquered my fear of thunderstorms for the most part. I used to be so scared of them I would go in the room with my sister during one, even in high school. Once she moved out, I started sleeping with the TV on. I no longer do that. When I had Aubrie, I had to pretend not to be scared for her. Then we got a dog that is horrified of storms. Aubrie and I both tried to be brave for her and both of our fears have lessened due to that. Unless it is so loud it makes you jump out of bed, it usually bothers me about as much as it bothers our other dog, who hardly notices it except in those cases.

One day, Aubrie was in the bath and it thundered so she jumped out. Our dog that fears thunder then jumped in not realizing the bath was full of water. She stood there stunned, trying to decide if she hated thunderstorms or baths more. After a few seconds she jumped out and licked herself dry for so long she forgot about the storm. The same dog ripped through a wooden door when we first got her trying to get into the bathtub when we were not home. She is only 32 pounds, but it looked like Beethoven had done it. It is crazy what fear can make you do and how much strength and adrenaline it can give even to a dog at times.

After all I have been through, I felt like I conquered all my fears until I had the first mouse in my house recently. I remember having a mouse once growing up and I got so scared I walked on the furniture until it was caught.

Apparently, we also had one years later, but my parents didn't tell me because I had freaked out so much the last time. At twenty-nine years old, I got my first mouse of my own.

At this point my husband wasn't living at home and I freaked out when I saw it, and immediately called my dad. He said that the mouse was more scared of me and I told him the mouse wasn't hyperventilating and shaking like I was. He probably was though once he heard me scream, poor thing. My parents helped me put down traps and patched up where we thought the mouse had come in. Aubrie and I stayed with them a couple days and still no mouse. Aubrie and I were ready to sleep in our own beds again, so we just assumed the mouse probably went out the way he came in before we patched it up, and we came back home.

The next day I was doing laundry. I put clothes into the washer, then as I put them in the dryer and looked down at what I thought was an empty washing machine, there was a dead mouse. You think I would be calmer since he was dead but not really. Thoughts raced through my mind about how that mouse got there. Did I carry him alive in my clothes and put him into the washer? Was he already in there dead or alive? Aubrie was not at all upset about the mouse. I tried to stay as calm as I could in front of her.

Aubrie wanted to keep him when she first found out. After this happened, she would just calmly tell people, "Mommy put the mouse in the washing machine and the mouse got dead." Well that about sums it up. So, I called my dad to come over from fifteen minutes away just to get that thing out of my washer. My stepdad would do anything for me. I try not to take advantage of that too much, but this was one of those times I was willing to. I just could not bring myself to do it. I felt bad for the mouse. Despite my fear, I hated he died such a rough death.

A few months later, Aubrie and I were walking through the pet store. We stopped to look at the hamsters, gerbils, guinea pigs, mice and rats. They were of course in cages and not loose in my house and for sure disease free. As I stared at them trying to ignore their nasty little tails, they looked so cute. Two of the rats were laying on each other just staring sweetly at us looking a little tired. The mouse was entertaining us playing on his wheel. I thought, "This is what I was so scared of?" I am not saying I have conquered that fear. I would probably still freak out if I saw one in my house right now. It is something I have had to deal with so little in my life I guess I am not as concerned about conquering it. It is the worst feeling to let something have that much control and power over you though.

I still have other fears including being a little claustrophobic. My husband helped me guide me through an unexpected claustrophobic part of a haunted house years back just so I would not have to walk backwards to the entrance. He held my hand and talked me through it. I once watched an episode of the show Fear Factor where you had to get zipped up in a plastic bag and put under water. You were supposed to unzip yourself and get free but if you had trouble someone was standing by to assist. That was one of three stunts those people had to do on the show just to have a shot at $50,000. Are you kidding me? I would not do that if you guaranteed me all the money in the world because I would panic and probably die in that bag. That is one situation where fear would still be a factor for me.

I used to love roller coasters when I was younger and fear those now as well. My husband used to fear them and now enjoys them. I started having a panic attack on a log ride years ago and did not even tell anyone when it was happening. I just tried some breathing techniques I knew might help and hung in there. I was fine once we went over the big drop at the top; it was of course just- anxiety. I used to go on roller coasters that went upside multiple times with my eyes open and arms up.

I doubt I will ever conquer all my fears, but I do try not to let any of them take control of my life like they did before. I used to worry all the time. If I didn't have something to worry about now, I would worry as far into the future as retirement. I don't even get as scared of horror films after all I have been through. I still feel like someone may grab my leg from under the seat sometimes when watching one in a theater but otherwise I don't get bothered much anymore by most of them. I don't really know why other than maybe for the first time for me, life was more horrifying than those scary movies.

Fear isn't always a bad thing though. In addition to praying to go to sleep and not wake up when I was during my depression, I also got to a point where I was no longer scared of eighteen-wheelers. I have always hated having to pass an eighteen-wheeler on the interstate, especially when they start to swerve into your lane when you are next to them. This would happen when I was really depressed and I would think, "Oh well, if it happens, it happens." I eventually got back to the point where I feared them again and that was a good feeling. After you go that far the other direction, you appreciate life so much more. You notice the moon and stars and sunsets and sunrises, and everything beautiful more than ever before and you want to live more than ever before. Food tastes better, everything is better, and even getting scared while passing an eighteen-wheeler can be viewed as a positive.

My own misconceptions about mental illness caused me to judge myself harshly as I was going through it. Was I just being selfish and lazy and using certain things as an excuse? I had never been like that before so why now? Was I just a bad person? Maybe I was. I had just had it easy before, so it was easy to praise God and be a good person but now that all these bad things happened, I cursed God and became this horrible person. I finally concluded that it didn't matter if this was my fault or not. I needed help. I didn't want to be like this anymore and it didn't matter if it took pills, therapy, or other things I was uncomfortable with to get better, I was going to do whatever it took.

Some people worry so much about whether mental illness is someone's fault or not. First, it is not. Now everything a person with mental illness does cannot be excused by the mental illness of course but maybe they need help to stop. If someone is hanging off a cliff because they weren't paying attention and tripped on a rock, are you going to leave them there and tell them it is their fault? Are you going to push them off because they are so stupid for getting them self in that situation? May sound crazy but that is the attitude some people take with depression. It gets even more complex when you try to help the person and they either blame you or say there is nothing wrong with them. Would you still leave that person hanging on a cliff?

The truth is you can try to help them, and they may end up falling anyways. However, the right thing to do is to still try and help them because they can't get up on their own. I guess people feel they will get pulled over the cliff too. Depression can be contagious, and it is often hard to be around people when they are depressed. It is depressing being around people that are physically ill too, and they are also usually contagious, but this does not stop them from getting help. Hopefully one day mental illness will be treated the same as physical.

I still take full responsibility for the things I did and said while depressed but for the first time in my life I dealt with a couple deaths, a layoff, a new baby and my husband leaving me all in a short time. I just didn't know how to handle it. I was overwhelmed and I needed help. Does it really matter that I handled things wrong or couldn't handle them? Did that make me a horrible person? No, it made me human. I was never the monster I thought I was, and I eventually realized that when I talked to so many others going through the same. I still took care of my daughter and did my job I just had some bad thoughts, said some bad things and had a horrible attitude. I was just unhappy and wanted so badly to be happy again. I was always the strong and positive one and for once I needed others to be strong and positive for me.

At one point during my recovery I came across boxes of keepsakes. They contained letters Jay and I had written to each other in high school and college, letters my friends had written me in middle school and high school and college, even one my real father wrote me in college, any thank you letters or cards I had received with meaningful messages, awards I received, newspapers I had been in, etc. Going through this box, reading so many great things said to me and about me really uplifted me. This is the person I was. Not the monster I had made up in my head over the last year or two.

In addition to therapy and pills I did many other things to get better. I researched to see what all my options were and what kind of stuff worked for other people. A lot of things ended up helping me: massages, blogging, talking to others and helping others who had been through the same, exercising, working less, asking for and accepting more help, doing some of my hobbies I used to enjoy more again, getting more sleep, making more time for myself, my friends and family, and spending less time obsessively organizing pictures and cleaning. I would update or change the pictures in our house so much that Jay finally pointed out to me once that no one had even come over since the last time I had changed them.

I finally realized that I was not taking care of me. I was taking care of everyone else and resented it because I was neglecting myself in the process. I watched my mother do that her whole life, so I thought that was what I was supposed to do. As I got older though I realized, that is what made my mother happy. She told me that herself. She always put us first and didn't have many friends or hobbies. She worked and took care of us and made sure we had homemade meals and a clean house. My sister and I didn't want that though. We wanted to still be able to have friends and time to ourselves and hobbies and dates with our husbands. We didn't want to give all of that up. What I gave up instead was having the perfectly clean house and organized pictures. I realized it was okay if my child sometimes ate pop tarts, cereal or fast food and didn't always have a home-cooked meal.

I did have to give up some things when I had a child, but I finally realized I had a choice as to what those things were. When Aubrie was first born, I did give up my hobbies and time to myself and time with my friends and husband. All I did was cook and clean and work and take care of her. I had to change that so I could be the best mother I could be to her and I wasn't doing that by being my mother. My mom was a great mom to me but because she was doing what worked for her and made her happy.

Chapter 3

The Myth of the Instant Bond

I learned so much about love going through what I did. I thought I knew everything about it, but I was wrong. I still don't know everything except that love, and life are both so complex. I have always been a romantic. You will often hear me compare my life to movies. I am one of those mush balls who believes in fairytales, or at least I used to be. Even the people who love this about me will sometimes get annoyed when I compare reality to movies and fairytales, but movies are often based on real life and even fairytales are not that far from reality. Most fairy tales include stepparents, villains, obstacles to overcome, but they also have a happy ending if you don't give up and if you aren't the bad guy.

In some of the newer cartoons my daughter likes even the villains sometimes turn good now and still have a happy ending. In others, some villains' children become heroes while some heroes' children become villains. Others show the villain's side of the story and how they became a villain. This often includes being mistreated by the heroes. I like these new versions of fairytales that I feel teach children that there are not good and bad people. We all have good and bad in us and we make choices every day to do good or bad. We can change those choices at any moment. We are also not defined by our parents or family.

As head in the clouds romantic as I was, I still have never really believed in love at first sight. I have heard people talk about it but never bought it, but now I think I understand what people mean. I had that kind of instant attraction and connection with a guy friend during my marital problems, which confused me even more. People talk about the same thing when they see their child for the first time. You just fell in love the first time you saw them.

I think it's a little different with your child though, which is why you hear about that kind of love at first sight much more often. If you are the mother, that child has been in your body for nine months. During that time, I talked to Aubrie, learned things about her personality and really enjoyed having someone with me all day. Of course, I felt bonded to her already when she was born. Or at least I think I did. I didn't have some magic emotional moment when she was born though like some people seem to have. When she was first born, I didn't even cry. My husband did but I was so tired because I had no epidural that I just said, "Hey baby". Five minutes later, I was on an adrenaline rush and I didn't feel like crying then either. She was my child and she was an adorable precious baby. It was easy to love her at that moment.

I met my husband when we were fourteen years old. It was not love at first sight. We became friends sitting next to each other in Biology and would even sometimes write notes to each other in class about the people we were dating at the time. I thought he was cute and funny, but I just didn't think of him like that at the time. We became closer later our sophomore year when I started playing soccer too. He would give me rides home because I didn't have a car yet. He had always been a big flirt, with every girl, not just me, and over time I began to flirt back. A friend finally told me he liked me, and I told her that I thought I liked him too. She told him and he eventually asked me out.

By the time Jay and I had been together eight months I already knew I wanted to marry him one day and was going to love him forever. I have always thought into the future. Jay was not like that, however. That was part of his appeal. I wanted to worry less and be more laid back like him and I think he wanted to be more thoughtful and responsible like me. Like most guys though, I don't think his plan was to meet the person he wanted to marry in high school. I have had other guys tell me since high school that they did not date me in high school because I was the kind of girl you marry, and they were still sowing their wild oats and did not want to hurt me.

I doubt Jay was thinking about marriage or children or any of that stuff eight months in. Even when we said our wedding vows seven years later, I was imagining him going through Alzheimer's or being bed ridden and me taking care of him and other worst-case scenarios. He was probably just thinking, "I love her now, I am happy now, and have been for seven years now. I will always be happy with her and love her". That is how most people think.

Other than a near break up one year of college because we were long distance and it was hard, and one time when I broke up with him after we had our first fight, things were smooth sailing for over ten years for us after we started dating. We had fights but we never had that point two or three years in or even seven years in where it got hard and we lost that in love honeymoon feeling. We decided to try for a baby shortly after our second wedding anniversary. We had Aubrie right before our third one.

By the time Aubrie was two years old and we had been together for twelve years, for the first time we had lost that in love feeling. Until I went through my depression, I never realized how much work I put into our relationship. It seemed like we were just soul mates and meant to be. When I became so overwhelmed with everything bad happening to me and trying to handle Aubrie during it, and wasn't really putting anything into my marriage anymore, it started to show. It turns out it was work all along.

My husband told me he was not in love with me anymore. He loved me but was not in love with me. This didn't really make sense because I knew he didn't love me like a sister. He was still attracted to me and other than not connecting lately that part of our relationship was never the problem. So, he was attracted to me and loved and cared about me but wasn't in love with me? What does that even mean? Looking back though I realize I did not feel in love with him anymore either. The truth was I didn't feel love towards anything anymore so my lack of love for him did not really stand out to me specifically. Not that I didn't really love anything or anyone, I just couldn't feel it. I felt numb. Not all the time but most of the time.

I didn't have that in love feeling with my husband, with Aubrie, with Auburn football, with anything most of the time. Luckily that all eventually returned, including my love for Auburn just in time for me to enjoy their National Championship win in 2010. Subconsciously or not, I think my husband and I both started working more to avoid home. I read a quote on *Facebook* today and I am not sure where it originally came from but it said, "Feeling the need to be busy all the time is a trauma response and fear-based distraction from what you'd be forced to acknowledge and feel if you slowed down." Once my husband and I both started working so much, Aubrie bonded with my mom more than either of us. She was with her so much since she kept her while we were working. Eventually my husband and I both bonded with her more as we made work life balance a priority.

Even though I was impatient with Aubrie a lot and was emotionless a lot when she was younger, she still seemed to get that I loved her. I took care of her every day and spent a ton of time with her. I hugged and kissed her and told her I loved her. Just because I didn't always seem super happy doing it did not matter to her. She didn't take it personally. My husband on the other hand did, even though what I was feeling or not feeling was not about him or even exclusive to him. It is easier to make kids feel loved than it is adults. Maybe it is because they are used to getting more unconditional love than we do so they are also better at giving it.

My husband left me because he thought it would make him happier, me happier and our daughter happier. I was not happy either, but I had put so much into our relationship I could not imagine throwing it all away and starting all over again because of one bad year. We had eleven good ones before that. I just did not understand how he could do this. I was also still going through depression and even told him I could handle depression and I could handle divorce but not both at the same time. I begged him to stay until I got better but he refused. Ironically, much later, at one point he came back fully committed refusing to leave no matter what and I wanted to leave anytime he did anything to make me unhappy. In the long run, our relationship changed just as we had changed as individuals. He was more committed, and I was no longer a mush ball who believed in soul mates.

I now know without a doubt that if anything ever happened to Jay or our relationship, I would be okay without him. I know I could be happy alone or with someone else, but I still choose to be with him anyways and the same is true for him. I have had so many people tell me that they never loved anyone else the same way they loved their first love once that person broke their heart. The same was true for me except I ended up back with my first love after we broke each other's hearts. I honestly think it is a much healthier kind of love you have for others after that.

When I worked in senior living, sometimes when the spouse of a resident would pass in Independent Living, they would have trouble surviving without them. Sometimes only one spouse handled finances, sometimes only spouse handles cleaning and cooking or sometimes one spouse handled everything. When that spouse passed, the other was lost. Sometimes they would pass soon after. People often think this is sweet and romantic and I used to as well but working in Senior Living and going through my marriage almost ending gave me a different perspective.

Sometimes seeing the independence gained over time after this happened by the spouse left behind was amazing. They were so dependent on the other person and were lost without them and that can be sad to witness. Most eventually made it okay on their own, even if they had a little help from other residents, employees, family or friends at first. This did not always happen though. Other times, the spouse left behind was not in good health mentally or physically and forever after that relied on help from friends, family and/or strangers. I can at least say where I worked, most of those strangers still treated them better than most people treat their own family.

Jay and I used to get in arguments even before Aubrie was born when we were long distance at one point and when our work schedules were opposite when we first got married. I was upset we did not have as much time together. I was upset when he could not come to family functions, work functions, friends' weddings, etc. with me. When we first started dating, we did everything together, but we were in high school and college so we could. Jobs, distance and eventually a child started to get in the way of that and it really bothered me a lot for a long time.

There are couples who seem to do almost everything together and had date nights, etc. even with kids and jobs and I wanted to be one of those couples like when we first dated. I eventually realized to become one of these couples I was either going to have to get a new husband, or my husband was going to have to change careers and go to a lot of events he did not want to go to. We have since come to a compromise. We both changed jobs and work less so that we have more couple and family time, and I finally enjoy time by myself more or time with friends or family without Jay when he can't be there. Maybe when we are empty nesters one day, we can get even closer to how it was in the beginning.

I totally get though why some people jump from relationship to relationship to keep that honeymoon feeling all the time or to get it back. It is a pretty great feeling. People say you can keep it going or get it back again, but once you are comfortable with someone it is never the same as that excitement with someone new. The comfort and trust you build over time are great too though and if you can have that and try as much as possible to keep the honeymoon stage alive, the combo of all of those is truly the best.

Even the best relationships you will have unhappy times and you can often work through these and be happy again as Jay and I have. I could find a lot of people easier to get along with than him. I could find someone just like me who agrees with me on everything but what would I need them for? I don't want to be married to myself. It is hard to be with someone that is opposite from you on a lot of things because you challenge each other to grow as people and learn from each other. You are going to learn some things about yourself you don't like, and you might have to change. It is especially harder when you fall in love as young as we did.

I know a lot of people who got together at the same age and split up later once they realized what they truly wanted out of a relationship at an older age. When this happens, you must decide if you can do without certain things in the relationship that you want or see if your spouse is willing to compromise and change some to accommodate what you need. No one knows what they need in a marriage when they are sixteen years old, which is when we started dating. We both ended up changing and sacrificing a lot and both learning to live without certain things. He now does things for me I never thought he would do, and I now do things for him I never thought I would do. When your marriage survives such a tough time, it can become stronger and better and as I write this, I truly think ours has.

My husband thought he was doing the right thing by leaving me. He thought he was doing the best thing for me and him and Aubrie since we were miserable. Even many who criticized him had done the same thing in the past or were married to someone who had done it to someone else in a previous marriage. Also, as someone recently told me, what happens between two people in their relationship is really no one else's business anyways. No one else knows every detail of your relationship or what is right or wrong for either of you more than you two do. Regardless, I found myself harshly judging people who left their spouses for years, even when their own spouse had forgiven them, and I had forgiven mine and even took him back. It was just the most painful thing I have ever been through. I eventually realized this though and reminded myself what that person recently told me anytime I caught myself doing this.

I blamed Aubrie and having a child for all my problems. Jay blamed being married to me for all his and it is a lot easier to get out of marriage this it is to get out of being a mother. The truth is I was good at hiding my Depression, Anxiety and OCD most of the day. I felt so comfortable at home around my husband and daughter that I let it all out there and only around them.

When you have a child, loving them is work just like loving your spouse is. Some will say different because you are blood, but think of how many blood relatives you are not close to at all. Think of how many people are not close to their parents or children at all. Think of how closely many stepparents and adoptive parents are bonded with their stepchildren and adopted children. If you have a baby and have no problems whatsoever before, during, or after having the baby then you might feel an instant bond and love that baby so much. They are so sweet and innocent at first. If you get married and everything before, during, and after getting married is wonderful, you may feel like you have found your soulmate or fell in love at first sight and feel constant love for that person. However, throw in some hard things to deal with like medical problems, deaths of loved ones and job layoffs and life gets hard. So does marriage and kids.

Bad things are always going to happen in life but when they happen right around the time someone is entering your life, unfortunately, that person often ends up taking the blame for most of it even if they had nothing to do with it. That is what happened when I had a child because all I knew was life was great and then I had a child and it wasn't. Of course, that wasn't how it was but at the time it seemed that simple.

When your child is first born you are just meeting them. You feel like they have no faults and are perfect and you love them so much and can't live without them. You want them to think you are perfect and you want to be perfect for them. As time goes on you see each other's faults and learn from them and forgive each other. You compromise and grow together and your love for each other grows into a stronger, deeper love. You go through hard times and sometimes, just like with your spouse, they drive you insane. You know deep down you love them, you just don't love how you feel in that moment.

When things get hard after you get married or after you have a child, sometimes you think, what in the world was I thinking? I made a mistake. I shouldn't have gotten married or I shouldn't have had kids, or I should not have married this person. Sometimes you blame the other person but sometimes it is your own insecurity. You think you are just not cut out to be a wife or a mother. It is harder than you thought. Well, the truth is that it is, but if it were easy it wouldn't be so wonderful and rewarding.

The most meaningful thing my husband told me in fifteen years of knowing him was at one point when we got back together amid trying to save our marriage. He pretty much told me that I annoy the crap out of him, but he still wants to be with me forever, even though it is hard. He said he would rather be annoyed by me than not be annoyed by anyone else. That is why I used to say we have *The Notebook* romance. We have had almost every fight in that movie. Our fights were the entertainment at the lunch table in high school.

I did feel bonded with Aubrie before she was even born but it eventually went away, and it eventually came back again but it was because I worked to get it back. I started taking better care of myself so I could be a better mother to her because I wanted to be. It was a choice. It was always a choice. I was letting my fear that I was an awful mother and didn't have a bond with my child decide that I was going to be an awful mother and not bond with my child. I fooled myself into thinking it was out of my control.

The funny thing is that I recently learned on a show I love called *Adam Ruins Everything,* that the instant bond between mother and baby is a new concept. Newborns used to often die so they were often not even named for the first year. People tried to avoid getting too close at first, in case they lost them. There are some pregnancy and motherhood "myths" I discovered were true during my pregnancy and after. I also discovered some were myths. The best discovery of all was that it is different for every mother and with every baby. Aubrie had a head full of hair, but I didn't have heartburn when I was pregnant. I did get the "nesting" instinct right before I went into labor. At nine months pregnant, I suddenly got the urge and energy to stay up until midnight cleaning the entire house, ate a chicken sandwich, and started getting back pains I soon realized were contractions. I've talked to others who had their nesting instinct but it's never in the exact same way.

I also felt like I gained mother's instinct after Aubrie was born. My best example of this is that I was a heavy sleeper before I had Aubrie, but after having her, her cry would always wake me up. Even her making a peep would wake me up, but I would still sleep through almost every other noise and any other baby or child making those same noises. So, some of these "myths" proved to be true for me, but the one about the instant bond turned out to more work than instant for me.

When I hold babies now, I am a lot more knowledgeable than I was when Aubrie was a newborn. Every baby is different, so I still don't know it all, but I am a lot more comfortable than I was. I guess that is how I thought it would be when I had Aubrie. I recently went to visit a friend who had just had her first baby. Aubrie and I took her some dinner. My friend watched in amazement as I held her baby, ate my dinner, helped get Aubrie's dinner and Aubrie's drink ready for her and got onto Aubrie for something she was doing wrong. I told my friend not to worry. She will eventually grow octopus' arms and an extra set of eyes too, but they don't come out with the baby.

Chapter 4

Just Buy Her a Dress and She'll Be Fine

From the time a woman is pregnant her life changes forever. When people hear that they normally think of the fact that you have the person living inside you that you bond with and that forever changes your life for the better. However, one other way it changes is that suddenly you are not just one person anymore. You can't even walk around in public without some stranger thinking they have the right to touch you without even asking because you have a baby inside you, and it fascinates them. They also think they now have the right to tell you how to raise this child that hasn't even been born yet even though they don't know you. They also know how you should give birth apparently and should have a say in this.

This doesn't stop once the baby is born. Everyone still thinks they can walk up in public and touch your baby without asking and that you should listen to them about everything: how the child's hair should be, what clothes they should wear, what they should eat, what you should be doing to prepare them for school. If they aren't potty-trained fast enough or don't seem smart enough for their age or tall enough or skinny enough or don't act well enough in their opinion, etc. you are going to hear about that too. I now realize everyone was just excited and trying to help, but when you have just become a new parent it can be overwhelming and make you feel like a failure. You eventually learn you can't please everyone, and you quit trying and just do your best.

Another thing that can be overwhelming is everyone doesn't just tell you what they think you should do when it comes to the baby. You are now the baby's mother so they have opinions about what you should do with your life. This is especially true when you are pregnant. I didn't get depressed when I was pregnant. I was one of those happy pregnant women that other pregnant women hated. I felt very bonded with Aubrie and talked to her all the time and couldn't wait to meet her. However, I now see some things that started then that did eventually affect me over time when combined with other things.

I never did anything I thought could be dangerous for my child when I was pregnant but that does not stop people from telling you how much rest you should be getting and what you should be eating, etc. You already feel these concerns have little to do with you and everything to do with the baby. This continues after the baby is born. It starts to feel like the only reason anyone is concerned with you is so you can care for the baby. A mother is a very important role in life but what about your other roles as wife, daughter, sister, friend, employee or just simply as a human being?

Some people, especially women who have been through this before, understand and try to think of the woman and give her attention when she is pregnant and when the baby is first born. I have heard someone make the statement before that they bought someone a new dress so they would not get Postpartum Depression. If only it were that simple. It is a nice gesture, but it would be nice if everyone was just aware of this happening, and constantly tried to give mother and baby both the attention they need, knowing that it would benefit both mother and child. This would not even require gifts or constant attention, just showing a legitimate concern for the person and making sure that they feel loved too.

It is so easy to love that little baby so much that you forget to give the mother the attention and love she still needs. Even after having the baby the mother normally gets less medical attention and less check-ups than the baby. She is expected to continue her normal everyday duties and care for a newborn while recovering. I did have one friend who was already a mom bring us dinner one night. Her and her husband did not even stay to eat with us, just long enough to drop off a home cooked meal and visit and it was enough to last more than meal. It was super helpful and thoughtful.

People always think the husband should step up and assist and notice if something is wrong with the wife and help her. Often, they do, but other times they are as affected as she is. Approximately half of men whose wives get Postpartum Depression will get depressed too. Your husband is your partner and what affects you affects them also. If you experienced deaths in your family and a layoff, they did to. They have a new baby too. They are also working and not getting any sleep. They also miss the time you two used to have together, and their life is completely changed too.

The only major difference is a woman's body is affected physically and hormonally so people use hormones as a reason that women get postpartum depression and men can't. A drop in progesterone has recently been linked as a possible major cause of Postpartum Depression and Anxiety. As I write this, the first drug was just approved by the FDA to specifically treat Postpartum Depression. The drug treats it by mimicking progesterone. I think there is some truth to this because even since I recovered, I have had issues with low progesterone and have experienced infertility and other health issues due to it.

For some reason my doctors never gave me the option of treating the low progesterone with actual progesterone or other options. They only offered me a drug to treat infertility. Although a friend of mine who is a midwife recently told me that the low progesterone was a symptom of something deeper, and still not the cause, so I remain somewhat stumped as I write this. Fertility drugs have a ton of side effects I was concerned about. The doctor's main concern seemed to be my infertility and not my major weight gain, major painful acne, lack of energy, and three-week periods every month.

I eventually had some luck treating some of the symptoms by getting back on birth control for a little while even though I wanted to get pregnant. I could not get back on the kind I was on before due to side effects I was starting to have. I never thought having a baby would totally throw off my hormones and body like this with no solution in sight still even as I write this. Although some of it is probably also due to all the years on birth control, the time after the baby when I was working too much and the long period of time I was not being treated for my OCD and Anxiety. When I was working a lot, any time I would slow down and take some time off I would get sick. I was okay if I did not stop.

I now try hard to work less, exercise more, get enough sleep, eat well, etc. I try to listen to my body more and go lie down when I feel exhausted for instance. Although, sometimes my OCD still tries to convince me that I need to clean or walk the dogs or spend time with Aubrie instead. If my husband is exhausted when he comes home from work sometimes, he will often take a nap or go to bed. I have learned to follow his lead. Of course, this is easier now that my daughter is older, but even when she was younger, I should have done this more the days my husband was home to help. Even now if I need to rest and he needs to handle something else or vice versa, we will help the other so they can rest.

If Postpartum Depression is caused by a drop in progesterone though, how come every woman who has a child doesn't get Postpartum Depression? The risk factors include genetic and environmental factors as well, such as a personal history of mood disorders or mental illness, a family history of mental illness, stressful life events during and after pregnancy, a traumatic birth and/or, depression or other mood disorders or mental illness during pregnancy, lack of emotional and social support, and sleep deprivation just to name a few of the most common. Therefore, some men get it too and in a lot of cases, if a woman has a lot of support and experiences less personal trauma around the time of birth, maybe it can be less severe or even prevented.

When Aubrie was first born my husband would watch her while I jogged to the pool, swam a couple laps, laid off to dry off and ran back. I loved this because I got to exercise, layout and have time to myself. My first Mother's Day gift was him paying for me and several of my friends to go see the first *Sex and the City* movie and dinner. My husband did help a lot when she was first born, and I took a whole twelve weeks maternity leave and it was wonderful. I think this is the reason I didn't get really depressed until later in the year when more bad things happened. As a result, my husband worked more and helped me less. I would nag him about it which drove him to work even more. Our marriage was not a good one anymore, so I blamed that on his job. He denied that so then I started to blame Aubrie, I blamed God, I would blame anyone but him. Until he left me one day, then I finally did blame him. I blamed everyone but myself.

As time went on, I realized the mistakes I had made too, but when I first began to realize his, I was so angry at him and I did not understand why everyone else was not too and why they were not worried about him as well. This upset some of our mutual friends. I wondered how they could they be my friends and be okay with him abandoning me when I needed him most, but they all abandoned me too. I worked things out with most of them eventually. The sad thing is, these were some of our closest friends many years before, but they were not anymore. Some were liberal, some were conservative, some were religious, some were not. Some were the ones who post about helping others with mental illness and looking out for people, but they did not do that for me when I was going through it. They were too worried about me embarrassing Jay or embarrassing them to help, or too busy with their own problems. They were simply annoyed by me and angry at me. Even if they did not realize I was going through it at first, even once they did, they did nothing to help.

I was reaching out to friends and family I used to be close to because I felt like I had no one else. I was pretty much begging for help and love and reaching out as people say to do but got rejected. Jay was my best friend and I am very close to my parents, but for the first time ever, they were not always the easiest to talk to. My grandfather and real father passing were hard on my mom as well. She was very close to her father, and she spent more time with my father than my sister or I ever did. He was her first love and the father of her children.

Normally we all take turns leaning on each other, but we were all dealing with a lot at the same time. My sister was there for me some, but she was working full time with children and has her own close friends. I even tried to stay with her the first night Jay left, and her household could not handle the lack of sleep caused by Aubrie. My parents had trouble with it at first too. I understood since sleep deprivation the last two years was contributing to my current troubles yet also probably being made worse by those troubles at the same time.

When you work full time and have a small child, you don't have a lot of time for friends. One couple that even hooked up at one of our game nights years back sent Jay a save the date for their wedding when we were split up. Once we got back together neither of us got invited to the wedding because they did not want me there. At one point I thought we might even be in their wedding. One of them was in ours but now I found myself not even welcome. The one in our wedding even once pretty much told me that my marriage was over, and that I needed to accept it and move on. It hurts so much to this day.

They probably never think twice about me, and I don't much about them anymore. Occasionally they show in a nightmare or something or someone reminds me of them, and it breaks my heart a little again each time. I even tried apologizing to them more than once after I was better and explaining I was not in my right mind. They would not even respond or acknowledge my existence, which was so painful. This made me feel more like the failure I thought I was. I was not worthy of their friendship so there must be something wrong with me. I must have done so much wrong or been such a horrible person that it was unforgivable since they would not even acknowledge my existence anymore.

They did send me a generic thank you note for the wedding gift I sent them despite not being invited. I tried explaining that even my parents and Jay did not know how to deal with me when I was going through what I did. That was almost ten years ago, and I have not heard from them since and they still have me blocked on Facebook. One cousin I reached out on my real Dad's side of the family never replied, and instead read the personal message I sent her in front of that entire side of the family I later found out. Her sister also never responded to me even though we were very close as kids. I have not seen her or been able to get in touch with her for years since. I could not even get them to respond to give me an address to send a Christmas card to. I eventually quit even trying.

I have some great childhood memories with my dad and his family. I have made peace with his family since his passing because I did not want to have the same regrets I did when he died. My parents were divorced before I was even born and my sister was just a toddler. We were just innocent children but would still somehow face pressure and guilt the rest of our lives for the rocky relationship we had with our father, like it was our fault instead of his, which I never understood. I now understand that having a child like my father was as hard and as confusing for my grandparents as it was for me and my sister having a parent like that.

One good thing about this experience is that I no longer waste my time chasing after people who don't want to be in my life. I think a lot of my OCD and perfectionism was thinking if I could just be perfect maybe I would finally get the love and attention I wanted from certain people. They were too busy dealing with their own lives and their own problems. They did not have time to deal with the fact that my whole world was crashing around me. Did they even care if I lived? If I had ended my own life before this happened would they have shown up as a loved one? Would they have not come because they were angry that I had done it, even though they seemed to have no care for me at all when I was alive?

I finally realized that for one, you cannot choose your family. Two, maybe I cared for these friends and family more than they cared for me and we were never as close as I thought. Lastly, I had grown as a person. I used to be harder on people myself. Maybe I had outgrown these friends and family members anyways. They only had me at my lowest point in life and before and would miss me at my best. That was their choice to make, but it still makes me sad to miss out on them because I loved them.

I am closer to some of my husband's family than my own family. This is another reason Jay leaving devastated me. I was losing them too. Sure, I would see them at graduations, Aubrie's wedding etc. and be Aubrie's mom, but that was it. I was so close to them that Jay worried they might side with me when he left which was silly. While they were sad for me and supported both of us as best as they could, they were his family and ultimately there for him first. Once we got back together, it took me a while to get as comfortable around them as I used to be. It had taken a while to get that comfortable the first time. Now I had been reminded they were not my family, and in some sense, things will never be quite the same as before. I also wondered if it were not for Jay and Aubrie, would they have never spoken to me again either for the way I acted while not in my right mind?

My husband and some of our friends didn't see how I did not see his leaving me coming. I didn't see it coming at all. Looking back, I do, but at the time it was like I was almost in a coma but awake. One day I woke up from the coma and my husband was gone. All this time I was wallowing in self-pity, life was still going on around me without me. I woke up and finally had to deal with the things I had put off dealing with for so long. I had a lot of catching up to do. I really was stunned when it happened.

I never thought of divorce, even though I was unhappy too. I never blamed my husband for that even though it seemed to him like I did. I thought of him as family and his family as my family. I never thought he would leave me. When he said he was going to my heart literally felt like it was breaking in half and I learned that was a real physical feeling. I had no idea. I learned heart ache was too because after he was gone my heart physically ached for him, true chest pain. Since we had been together for so long, I had never felt either before. I finally related to and paid more attention to every song about a broken heart.

I had what I thought was a broken heart in high school and middle school but nothing like this-nothing like losing the father of your child and husband you were supposed to spend the rest of your life with-the person who was your best friend and you thought was your soul mate. I went through the physical symptoms of grieving a death. My doctor told me divorce was harder on most people than death of a spouse. That made sense to me. I kept thinking that would be easier because at least it wasn't their choice to leave you and you still felt loved. Also, when your spouse leaves you everyone you know doesn't come to visit bringing flowers, meals, hugs, help and advice, although some did. I did have several people check on me and even take me out to eat. I had so many say they wish they had known how depressed I was, but as soon as I got better, we went back to hardly seeing each other. I get it, life is busy, but what they did still meant a lot and made a difference.

I remember the day Jay left in bits and pieces like most things then. He probably remembers things differently than I do. I remember being up with Aubrie because, as usual, she would not sleep. I think I had to be up for work in about four hours. I could not wait for Jay to get home to offer me some relief. He was closing that night. I would often get excited at the sound of the garage door opening. That night, Jay texted me that he was going to Waffle House with some coworkers before he came home. This upset me and that upset him. I am pretty sure at this point he said he could not take it anymore and that he was leaving. He left on the same day he had asked me out twelve years before.

He had tried to leave a couple months before, which totally shocked me. We had our first date night in a while, and he told me he wanted to leave me. He had never mentioned leaving before, that I recalled. That was the day my heart broke and I begged him to stay. It took a lot of convincing him. At first, he told me that there was no chance in fixing us and it was too late. A year or two ago, we were fine. We were fine for at least ten years before that. How could we be so bad now that there was no chance of working things out, and this is the first I knew of it?

I think he was upset that I acted like this was the first I knew of it. I think in his head I had already left him mentally. Based on past conversations I have had with him I think by this point he had already mourned the loss of our relationship. He had already felt guilty for so long for wanting to leave and already made his decision and moved on. That is why he left and came back so many times before we worked things out. Any time I did anything that made him unhappy he used it as an excuse to affirm his decision.

I do remember him getting so upset one night when he called me. I think his car would not start. He needed me to drive thirty minutes to his work downtown in the middle of the night to give him a ride home. My initial reaction was how I was going to do this since Aubrie was sleeping. Any new parent knows the fear of waking a sleeping baby or toddler. I was also convinced by my parents to fear going downtown alone at night which Jay has always thought was ridiculous.

Jay probably remembers this differently as well, but I don't remember telling him no or that I would not come get him, but just seeing if a coworker was an option or if there were any other options. If there were not, I was not going to leave him stuck downtown. I was just trying to express my concerns to him, but he was so hurt and acted like he felt like he could not count on me in his time of need. It was so crushing to him. I had a weird response to him spending a lot of money on weight loss stuff and he accused me of being unsupportive. Everything I did was met with anger and overreaction.

I guess I did this for so long he was taking his turn. Maybe I was still doing it, but in retrospect, it honestly feels like during this time I had stopped or at least slowed back down and gotten somewhat back to normal. I feel like I was getting better at this point without ever even realizing there had ever been anything wrong with me. Now I was dealing with how all of what I went through affected him. That is why when he first left; I thought maybe something was wrong with him and not me. I regressed when he left though so then everyone could only see something wrong with me. I started to see there was something wrong with me too once I started journaling and piecing everything together from over the last three years.

Now that Jay was leaving, I was angry that I was going to have to raise Aubrie as a single mother. I wanted to run away to the beach the day he left, and I thought about it. I knew Jay believed I would not do it, so I wanted to prove him wrong and to make him and everyone else worry. I could not go through with it. I could not do that to my work, to my family and friends. Even in this state I thought too much about consequences. I was so tired of thinking about consequences. I think I even drove down the street at one point and came back before I left the neighborhood.

I didn't sign up for this by myself. It was even Jay's idea to have a child earlier than we had originally planned. I was hoping Jay would take Aubrie with him. I even asked if he wanted to, meaning just for a night or two for me to get over the fact he was leaving me. He said he would get her later in the week. I was a mess. I was acting like this and he was going to leave her with me? That was the moment I realized he still expected me to be her main caregiver. I just wanted him around more and now he was leaving for good. I decided to stay with my parents and get some help. I eventually went to the doctor, I started going to church again, and I started therapy. Once Jay finally realized what was wrong with me, he started trying to work things out with me and started helping more with Aubrie. We would end up being on again and off again for the next year and a half.

I would research about others going through the same and how to get your husband back. Most of the advice involved acting like you didn't care. Unfortunately, that was not possible for me at the time in my current mental state, but eventually it was easy to do since I stopped caring. It turns out they were right, he wanted me back then. My relationship felt like a Taylor Swift song full of games being played. At times he would tell me and everyone else there was no chance of working things out and the next moment we would be working things out. This did not help make me look less crazy to some of our family and friends at the time, including the friends I eventually lost. It also definitely did not make me feel less crazy.

I didn't want to get out of bed every day, but I did for Aubrie. I knew she needed me. At times I would almost convince myself she would be better off with my parents and Jay and that everyone else could take care of her, but deep down I knew no one could ever replace her mother. At first, I got better for her, but then as time went on, I wanted to get better for me, my friends, family and eventually, even for Jay.

I felt like when I lost myself Jay lost himself too. I was still angry at him for abandoning me when I needed him most, but before all of this we never experienced anything hard. We had it easy. We were still kids and then in a matter of two years we experienced a new baby, two deaths and a layoff. Neither one of us knew how to handle it. Amid us trying to work things out, Jay even lost two of his grandparents. He does now admit if he had handled things better in the beginning it might have saved both of us from making a lot of mistakes. However, he can't go back and undo it all and neither can I. If we could, I wouldn't be writing this book right now. We can only learn from it and do better going forward. That is all any of us can do.

Chapter 5

This Isn't the Kid I Ordered

      I never went to a birthing class. I didn't because people had told me they did and that it did no good. I now realize that is because most people end up having an epidural and/or get induced or have a C-section and I did none of the above. I decided to try with no epidural because I had talked to people who had given birth both ways. They said that even though it hurt a lot more without one, their labor was faster, and they recovered faster. Some had done it on purpose and some just didn't get to the hospital on time.

      I was also worried about back problems from the epidural because I already had a pinched nerve from falling down the stairs years before. I also figured that no epidural was healthier for the baby. If I have more children, I really want the epidural next time. I did a lot of yoga and walking during my pregnancy and that helped, but a birthing class would have helped more. During labor, I almost passed out from breathing so heavy and Aubrie came out breathing heavy but was okay. She had to be monitored for a short time in the transition nursery due to this though.

      At times during my pregnancy they told me Aubrie was so big that a C-section or induction might be in my future but luckily, she came on her own. I had heard so many horror stories about both that the thought of either scared me. Most I knew who had been induced ended up laboring all day and then had to have a C-section and endure both. An induction requires another drug with more possible side effects for both mother and baby, and a C-section is surgery. I had never had surgery.

Luckily, Aubrie was born three and a half weeks before her due date but perfectly healthy at eight and a half pounds. She would have been ten pounds had she come on her actual due date. My husband was almost ten pounds when he was born so maybe she was supposed to be ten pounds. Her original due date was May 1st then they changed it to May 17th and she was born on April 28th. Other than the heavy breathing, Aubrie had no problems and didn't even look like a newborn. She was so alert and had great color and a head full of beautiful hair. She had her first hair cut around six months old.

When we went to get the ultrasound where we found out Aubrie was a girl, it was a shock because we expected a boy. Not necessarily wanted a boy but expected one. Why? For at least the last four generations in my husband's family the first born had always been a boy. My husband goes by a nickname, but his full name is a IV. His great-grandfather, grandfather and father were all still alive waiting for that name to be passed down. His great-grandfather was over ninety-years old. During the ultrasound Jay jokingly asked why his son had a vagina? When we were told we weren't having a V, you could already see that look in my husband's eyes. You could tell he was thinking that his great-grandfather could pass at any moment and the chances of having his namesake before then were now even lower.

You could also see the fear in my husband's eyes with thoughts of her dating and doing girly things he did not understand. I assured him that he had sixteen years before dating. At the time I did not know she would get a boyfriend in Kindergarten that would last until sixth grade. I also assured him that as a little girl I not only played with dolls and played tea party, I also climbed trees, played video games and football, etc. If she was a girly girl who didn't even do any of that I didn't know what I was going to do with her either. She turned out to be a prissy tomboy, a lot like I was. I usually like surprises, so I was excited about having a girl. I did have a fear of fixing her hair and painting her fingernails, two things I am still not even that great at doing but have gotten better at thanks to her.

I always imagined us having a boy first or maybe even two boys just like my husband's parents had. I imagined a little red-headed boy that was laid back like my husband. Even when we found out we were having a girl I still imagined her with red hair and laid back for some reason. On that same ultrasound, we saw her sleeping with her hand on her face like I do. This might have been the first sign that I should have been more prepared for her to have more of my traits than I had recently imagined.

For some reason I never imagined a girl who talks all the time like I do and looks like me. When she makes certain faces, she looks just like Jay and she gets flushed sometimes like him and most redheads, but because she has my hair and complexion otherwise, most people say she looks just like me. She only had a red tint for a short time as a baby and not even when she was first born. I never would have imagined a girl that looks like Jay with my hair would turn out to be so beautiful. She also has a lot of traits like her Daddy. I had hoped that one of these would be being laid back like him so she would never worry the way I do. She is laid back in some ways and more like me in some others, but maybe it will be enough for her to worry less than I do.

On the same ultrasound where we found out Aubrie was not a boy, they thought it looked like there might be something wrong with her kidneys. They wanted us to have more ultrasounds done to keep an eye on them. It turned out to be nothing but then they wanted us to have more to keep an eye on her size. As I mentioned earlier, she was much larger than average and was predicted to be

10 pounds by the time I was full-term. That ended up just being more unnecessary worry.

The night I went into labor, I was at home and had just finished cleaning the entire house and it was midnight. Again, I should have known something was up because I was nine months pregnant and I suddenly had the energy and the urge to clean the entire house. As soon as I finished cleaning, I started to eat a chicken sandwich and started to feel back pain. I figured it was from cleaning. Then, I realized it was coming and going and thought that maybe I should start timing it. I then realized it was four to five minutes apart. I called my mom to make sure she thought I was in labor and she did. I then called my husband back and he was already on his way home from work. I had called him earlier telling him I might be, but I wasn't sure yet.

By the time we were leaving the house, I was sure I was in labor because I was leaning against the wall. By the time we called the doctor to let him know we were on the way, the contractions were two to three minutes apart. We got to the hospital at 2am and the main entrance was closed, and we were having trouble finding the other. I was worried that I was going to have her in the parking lot. We finally found the entrance and I was already 5cm by the time we got there but did not have her for another eight hours.

My husband, his mom, and my mom all stayed the whole time. My sister came in at the beginning, but she had to leave because they said there were too many people in the room, even though she had that many with her in the same hospital. When my sister walked in and realized I hadn't had an epidural she said, "When you said natural, I just thought you meant not a C-Section." The doctor's office I went to had you see all the doctors in case yours was not the one on-call when you went into labor. My doctor was the one who had delivered my nieces and he was not the one on-call. The one who looked like a young Tom Cruise was. I thought, "Oh no! Not the really cute one!" Yes, at this point I still cared. Later, I could have cared less if it was Tom Cruise himself. He had at least apologized to Brooke Shields by this point. Sorry, but I could not resist a Tom Cruise reference in a book about postpartum mood disorders.

I also had my toenails done because I cared at one point. The last thing I was thinking about when a bunch of strangers were standing around me in that position, while I was in the worst pain of my life, was my toenails. A lot of women also worry about pooping while giving birth. I honestly don't remember if I worried about it and honestly don't even know if I did. I am pretty sure my husband may have hinted that I did at some point without coming straight out and saying it. I was in the room with my sister when she had my second niece. All I remember is after the baby came out, I turned around to not see what else came out after which is usually a combination of blood, afterbirth and probably poop and pee.

Luckily, halfway through, my doctor came on duty, so the same one who delivered my nieces, delivered Aubrie. Since I had seen one of them delivered, I really trusted him. Plus, how many people can still say that their kids and their sisters' kids were delivered by the same doctor? I have gone to the same doctor, dentist, and hair lady since we moved here when I was twelve. I am very old fashioned and always joke that I was born in the wrong generation.

The first thing my doctor said when he walked in was, "Why does she look like she is in so much pain?" Meanwhile I am thinking, "I am not supposed to look like I am in pain?" Then he said, "Oh, she didn't have the epidural." He had forgotten that I was going to try that.

Even the nurse in there with me had never assisted when an epidural had not been given. It is very rare apparently. As they monitored Aubrie, she had the hiccups as she often did when I was pregnant. That was how my husband felt her move for the first time.

I had no complications during birth other than a very painful leg cramp. Talk about two bad pains in one! At one point the nurse said, "I think she is in more pain from the leg cramp than the contractions." I was thinking that I am and to please make it stop. Like I mentioned before I almost passed out from breathing too heavy towards the end and was also screaming, "I am so stupid I should have had the epidural!" I wanted it at the end as the baby was coming out, kind of like in the movie *Knocked Up*. Everyone kept telling me how great I was doing, and I kept saying and thinking, "No, I am going to die, I am going to die."

As my labor progressed, I also got to the point I didn't want anyone touching me anymore. My husband was trying to rub my head and my back, and I loved it at the beginning. At some point it became agonizing to bear. I eventually snapped at my poor husband like you always see portrayed in commercials and TV shows and movies. He was just trying to do anything he thought he could do to help at the time. I had back labor the whole time. The most painful part was as she was coming out, but I was able to push through it because I knew it was almost over. I felt more relieved than I ever have in my life when it was over. I was in labor for ten hours, which is short for a first labor, but afterwards it felt like it had only been five minutes. It felt like I had been dreaming. I guess that is how women do it again.

I was so tired that all I could say was "Hey baby" as I finally saw my baby for the first time. Even though they say the baby isn't supposed to come out hungry, she did.

71

My mom said it was because I fed her constantly when she was in there and then starved her for ten hours while I was in labor. I usually snack or eat every couple of hours. To this day, Aubrie does too. She came out with the bird mouth going. I remember getting very excited at the point I realized Aubrie already recognized me as her mother. The day she was born I went to see her in the nursery. She stopped crying as soon as they handed her to me. She started to cry again as soon as they took her away. People tell you that babies know from your voice and smell, but it was still amazing to see.

The nurses would ask me if I needed pain medication and I would tell them I was just fine. I was on a high from the adrenaline from not having an epidural and I felt great! I laughed when the nurse thought she had hurt me pulling off a Band-Aid and apologized. I was thinking, "Are you kidding me? Did you see what I just did?" It also helped that everyone was amazed by what I did and made me feel like Superwoman. I felt as if I could handle anything after that.

I didn't even attempt to breastfeed because I thought it would give me anxiety, since I get stressed easily and that would be bad for the baby. I used to get stressed even just being around other people trying to breastfeed who were getting stressed out themselves. I think I will at least give it a try next time. Regardless, Aubrie has turned out to be very healthy.

One downside to having an epidural is you go from feeling nothing to everything. When you don't have it, you go from feeling everything to the aftermath, which is nothing compared to during. It still wasn't easy though. Although I have some family members and friends who were nice enough to share some of the aftermath of birth with me, no one really tells you that you will be carrying a kit to the bathroom for about two weeks. That is if you are lucky. I was lucky to not get a lot of stretch marks anywhere most people could see, but it turns out that isn't the only the only thing you can get while pregnant that doesn't ever go away. Some women get hemorrhoids too and apparently those never ever go away-ever. They only flare up at certain times, but certain times for the rest of your life. You can sometimes correct with surgery, but this is pointless until you are done having children and can be very painful. The same goes for any bladder leakage after, which a lot of women experience.

I was at least warned that a lot of women's hair starts to fall out after you have a baby. The reason it is important to be warned about this is that the reason it happens is that you lost less hair while you were pregnant due to your estrogen levels being up. Once they go back down, your body sheds that extra hair and you start to find it all over your bathroom. Luckily it eventually stopped, and I didn't go bald. Turns out you don't always have the same things happen to you that happened to your family and friends. When I was pregnant, I almost passed out one time. That had never happened to my mom or sister, so I called the doctor's office and turned out it happens to other women and is normal. I found out after that it happened to others I knew.

When we found out we were having a girl, I loved so many girl names I had to narrow it down. Most of the family seemed to like Aubrie. I even put up names on a baby blog website I had and let everyone vote and the winner was Aubrie Lynn. Her middle name is the same as her Daddy's mother because Aubrie was her first grandchild. Aubrie was chosen because it was a pretty name and because it was like the name of the college, and town I fell in love with at eighteen years old. We also thought she might have red hair like her Daddy's which is sort of Auburn colored. She did have a red tint for a little while as I mentioned before, but it eventually faded away as she got older. When she was first born her brown hair was so dark it looked black and she had a tan. The jokes began about the milk man because my husband is a pale redhead.

She didn't look like my husband at first. She looked like me but even darker hair and skin. She eventually started to look like him and he was so happy when she did, not because he really thought she was the milk man's, but because I think everyone wants their child to look or act like them in some ways. They want to get pleasure out of seeing a part of their self being passed onto the next generation, hence the reason a name being passed on means so much. My stepdad and I are not even blood but because he raised me, I act like him in some ways.

Jay's mom was with us the day we found out Aubrie was a girl and she was thrilled! She had two boys and now she finally had a little girl she could buy stuff for and do girly stuff with! It wasn't long before Aubrie won the heart of his dad over too. Growing up he was tough on the boys as most good fathers are. Most people are tougher on their kids than their grandkids and men are also usually tougher on boys than girls.

The boys knew they were not supposed to talk when their dad was watching TV. Aubrie talks the entire time her Pop-Pop is watching TV and it does not seem to bother him one bit. Even if it did, I would love to hear how he stopped her because I haven't found a way yet. Even before Aubrie came along, when I started taking trips with Jay's family, they were used to trips with few stops to eat or use the restroom, and not much talking in the car. They were used to boys.

When I married into the family, I was used to eating every two hours, and was brought up to never hold it when I need to go to the bathroom because my great-grandmother died of kidney disease. You can bet that the father who hardly ever had to pull over with his boys didn't hesitate to pull over for his daughter-in-law and granddaughter. I do talk less while in the car with his family, but for me, talking less is still talking more than they normally do.

Now, when Aubrie is in the car too, I can hardly get a word in myself. When my husband and I were separated I joked that my test for the next guy would be if he could make it on a long car trip with both me and Aubrie without jumping out of the car. These two girls coming into the life of two parents who had two boys changed things for them. It meant the world to me at our rehearsal dinner when Jay's parents called me the daughter they never had. Little did they know at the time that they would eventually get a mini version of me in a grandchild.

Aubrie did not look or act like we imagined. She wasn't even a boy like we imagined, yet somehow, she was better than anything we could have ever dreamed. She didn't only steal Nana and Pop-Pop's hearts she stole her Daddy's and everyone else's. She was also the first grandchild that was a Granny's baby. Her Granny is my mom. All the other grandkids were Pawpaw's babies. Aubrie was not the first grandchild on my side because I am the baby in my family while Jay is the oldest. All the other grandkids followed my stepdad around and loved to help Pawpaw fix stuff around the house and wash his truck and ride in his truck, etc. Pawpaw was the one who gave them attention while Granny cooked and cleaned.

Pawpaw tried so hard for her attention at first, but she didn't want it. She wanted Granny's and boy did she get it. My mom finally got her first Granny's baby like she had always wanted. Granny is usually so busy that I guess Aubrie feels special if she can break her away from cooking and cleaning and get her attention. Pawpaw has finally learned how to get it himself. Since he has had to work harder for it, I think it almost seems more rewarding. My stepdad must act like he doesn't want her attention and then she gives it to him. It also helped when he recently bought a new truck. My child was the fifth grandchild on that side, but they are all so unique, because just like the others when they came along, she was different from all the rest.

Aubrie was not the laid-back redheaded boy we imagined. Maybe the next one will be, maybe not. As I was writing the first volume of this book, Jay's great-grandfather was still alive at ninety-six years old. However, when Aubrie was two years old his son, Jay's grandfather passed away unexpectedly. The whole time we were worrying about his great-grandfather not meeting the V, we never thought about his grandfather not meeting him. Two months later Jay's grandmother passed also, and to this day I believe from a broken heart. A while after that, his great-grandfather passed as well before I started Volume 2. However, both got to meet Aubrie and are in pictures with her. We also have pictures of her with the four generations before. Her gender and name do not take away from how amazing that truly is.

Chapter 6

The Imperfect Out-of-Control Life of a Perfectionist
Control Freak

If you want to see a time that TV portrays
Postpartum Depression accurately, watch the movie *Marley
& Me*. Although, if you are depressed and/or you have lost
a dog you are close to before, you might not be able to
handle the end. There is also a part relating to a
miscarriage that may be hard for some to watch. Despite
losing my family dog growing up, I have still been able to
watch it several times, and it is probably even one of my
favorite movies, but this is different for everyone.

There are about ten minutes of that movie that deals
with the wife in the movie getting Postpartum Depression.
She acted exactly how I did when I had it, and her and her
husband had the same fights Jay and I did. This wasn't the
usual TV portrayal of a woman crying constantly, acting
depressed or just completely losing her mind. This was a
wife and mother who, before she was depressed, was her
husband's dream woman.

The wife in the movie was thoughtful, she was
beautiful, she was a planner, and a hard worker. She was a
good wife and a good mother. She loved animals and
children. She was a woman who eventually learned, after
going through PPD, that the greatest things in life are the
things you don't plan at all. She eventually quit all that
planning. This was a woman who changed after they had
their second child and wasn't a pleasure to be around
anymore.

The one part I related to most is when she finally gets the kids down for a nap and lays down on the bed herself after being so stressed. She starts to get relaxed and she hears the garbage truck. At that moment, she knows the dog is about to hear it and start barking and wake up the kids. When he does, she absolutely loses it. She yells at the dog and screams and gets the children even more upset. I believe her husband walks in at that point and gets more upset too.

The part that best describes how I think my husband felt is when she is getting onto her husband for not being home helping enough. She goes on about how hard things are for her and he replies by saying something like "because it is so much fun coming home to feel like part of a chain gang". The husband sits in the car at one point not wanting to walk in the house when he comes home. The husband had no clue what was going on, until his boss brought up the possibility of it being PPD when he was venting about things at work.

The movie was based on a true story and a book, so it portrays what the author and his wife went through which must be why it is so realistic. A lot of time when PPD is in a movie or show it is an extreme case of Postpartum Psychosis displayed in the form of a horror or drama. I would love if this book took off and turned into maybe a romantic comedy to show more people that PPD happens to normal people and they can get through it and get better. It can just be a tough moment in your life you overcame. It does not have to end tragically.

My husband knew something was wrong, but he didn't know what or how to fix it. Looking back, I can now see that during my depression, when we would go on a trip and had fun my husband would want to move to the town we visited. When we went to a movie and enjoyed it, he would want to go see it again. It was like he wanted to capture that moment forever, but he couldn't. Things would turn bad again soon after.

My husband had the right idea. Time away, just the two of us, was part of what I needed. During those times I felt like me again and it felt like us again. I wasn't just a mother or an employee, I was me again and I was a wife. I got to have fun and while on trips with him I didn't have to worry about cooking or cleaning or taking care of Aubrie. If more of that had started earlier it might have even done the trick, but I was so far gone by this point. I needed some real help. Our parents were close by, but they kept Aubrie so much while we were working that we normally had her when we were not. If we didn't it was usually only long enough to sleep in or take a nap or maybe go to a movie or dinner. Because the grandparents were not far away, she never went any anywhere for more than a night or two or a couple of hours.

Although what happened over a couple years of my life was summed up in only 10 minutes of *Marley & Me*, it summed it up so well. The wife in the movie tells her husband that no one tells you how hard marriage and being a parent is or how much you must give up. She says no one prepares you for it. They try to but you don't get it or don't listen. She goes onto to say how she has given up so much of what made her who she was to be a mom and a wife. She feels like a bad person for saying it, but her husband tells her it's okay because he feels that way sometimes too. She goes on to say that despite how hard it is she made a choice. She does not regret it and they will just get through these things together, and he agrees.

I wish I had seen the part of *Marley & Me* between when the husband finally realizes his wife needs help and when she ends up eventually being okay again, but that part of the movie doesn't exist. I always say the same thing about the movie *The Notebook*. When are they going to come out with the movie that shows the time between when they decided to be together forever and when they died together at ninety? How did they do it?

Through my recent trials I have finally started to conquer my perfectionist control freak OCD issues like the character in the movie. I had a great childhood and a great family, but my family was a broken family. Even though they get along now, when my sister was a teenager she would fight with my stepdad, and when my stepbrother was a teenager he would fight with my mom. I didn't want to cause any more problems for any of them, which is why my mom probably called me the child every mother prays for, and why she was so shocked when I went through all of this. My brother also jokes now that we are grown up, that I was the Switzerland in the family, always neutral and trying to keep the peace. I tried to stay out of trouble because my parents already had enough to deal with.

I was also apparently born with the desire to do things for others. When I was a small child and my mom would take me to the store, if my siblings weren't there, I would try to get something for them too. She said neither one of them ever did. I also wanted to one day rescue all the dogs from the humane society and have a huge dog farm. Having this giving gene is something you must keep under control, so you don't give all your money or time away and eventually get burnt out. Even now I still constantly struggle to not put everyone else before myself. I don't want the dogs to do without a walk or for Aubrie to do without something just because I am tired.

It is a constant struggle to prioritize, but sometimes I realize me resting or being on time somewhere just might be more important at that moment than walking the dogs. I always think of planes when they tell you that you must put your oxygen mask on before you start trying to help others. A lot of times while doing something for someone else, I will realize how much I need it myself. When we go our first dog and I started walking her as much as possible because it helped with her anxiety, I realized how much it also helped with mine. I have always struggled with this at work as well.

Every employer I have ever had, intentionally or not has taken advantage of my OCD. I sometimes get so much work done in such a short amount of time my reward is normally more work. This often resulted in raises or promotions but always just a little compared to how much more work I was doing. I was once accepted 2k more a year to continue doing my job and to take on my boss's job as well when she left. I know what a naive sucker I seemed like. However, at the time there were regular layoffs in that company, and I had survived many already. At the time, I looked at as an opportunity to get more experience while making myself more of an asset.

I eventually asked for more money and got a little more. I eventually was laid off anyways. Once I took maternity leave, they realized they could do my job without me. The only reason was because I had done so much before I left and saved everything I could until I returned. I also left as many notes as possible in my absence and trained my replacement well. I was told by many that still worked things that never got done properly or at all once I was gone, or even when I was on leave. They could not lay me off right when I came back, of course, and I did not even go in the next mass layoff. They kept me around one more month so that I could lay off everyone else first and handle their unemployment claims and severance packages. This would have upset me more if they had not given me the same severance package.

Once, I left another job due to being overwhelmed and was replaced with two people. If I had just gone home when the work was done, they probably would have just hired that second person when I was still there. I realize now how much of this I unintentionally put on myself. After I got laid off from my first job though, I really started to fear not being such an asset to the company that they would not lay me off. My doctor once told me one symptom of OCD is thinking that the other people around you are slacking. I did think this at one point, but now realize that most other people were just smart enough to not stress themselves out so needlessly, and to kill themselves for everyone else around them, or for a job that will quickly replace you. This is also why it was hard for me when I did not feel I got the same in return from others, when I went through the hardest time of my life.

In my last job, I had a boss who brought out the worst in everyone, including me. Even on medication my OCD became worse because of her micromanaging and it is the only time I had a panic attack on medication. I eventually left that job, a job I had loved for years before under a different boss, for my mental health and it was a very hard but good decision. I could easily write another entire chapter or book called This Isn't the Career I Ordered. All I went through eventually made me a lot easier on other people and myself and made me realize that no job is worth your mental health.

I used to have a friend that was anorexic, and I never understood when people used to say that it was not about being skinny and was about control. When I would clean my house, it wasn't about my house being clean, it was something I felt like I could control, but the more I tried to control everything the more out of control everything got. The more I tried to perfect everything the more imperfect it became.

About six months before my husband left, I caused us to be an hour and a half late for Christmas dinner with some of his family. If you had asked me to describe what happened that night at the time, I would have told you that I was getting Aubrie ready all by myself while having to get myself ready and get everything else done. What really happened was Jay got Aubrie ready and he had everything packed and ready to go. He waited on me for an hour and a half because instead of getting ready, I was vacuuming and washing dishes. Even though we were going to someone else's house, for some reason it was so urgent that I get it done right away. When we would have people over, sometimes I would not be ready when they showed up because I would still be cleaning. I would sometimes even notice a cobweb I had missed and knock it down while guests were over. I started planning so much I never enjoyed the moment. There is a Billy Joel song I really related to at this point my life called Vienna that I encourage you to listen to if you can relate.

My OCD seemed to serve me well when I was younger. My OCD has helped me graduate from college in only three years with honors, start a 401k at 21, own a house by the time I was 22, manage a department by the time I was 25 but I couldn't handle being a mother? I felt like a failure. My doctor told me it was normal for people with OCD to excel in school but then to eventually struggle with marriage and kids. You can get perfect grades in school, but you cannot be a perfect parent or spouse. You also eventually burn out from trying so hard to be perfect. I also struggled with this at work since it is not exactly like school either. I have gotten raises, promotions or other rewards at times for working hard, but in the corporate world it is not the same as school. Other things factor in such as who you know, whether certain people like you or not, timing and luck just to name a few. Excelling at work also often takes sacrificing your personal life which I never had to do for school.

My OCD is why I am writing this book. A lot of it is pulled from blogs and journals I wrote while recovering. So even writing this book is therapy. Part of me still felt like I would not be completely recovered until it was finished. I am working on volume 2 now. When I wrote Volume 1, I was still recovering, and that book honestly probably should have been a journal. A lot of the same stuff is in Volume 2, but with less personal opinions and rambling about unrelated things, and more paragraphs and commas.

The truth is I have changed so much in the years since I first published this book. Seven years later, my religious and political beliefs have changed. I am not going into them in this book because they both divide people so much. People of all beliefs go through hard times in life as I did, and I want all of them to be able to get something out of this book. I have always had an open mind and will continue to, but going through all I did, I eventually realized what my own beliefs were as opposed to what I was just raised to believe. I truly found myself and became more comfortable being myself and sharing my true feelings without shame. I will just say that if your religious or political views are affecting your mental health, you might want to take a deeper look at them. Maybe you simply have some of them because your parents did, and their parents did and so on.

When I first got on medication for my OCD and Anxiety, I eventually weaned off too early, thinking I did not need it anymore. Eventually I realized I needed to get back on it. I no longer had any major stress in my life at the time. Things were good with my husband and me, with Aubrie, with work but I still did not sleep well, and I woke up in the morning with this sense of dread to start my day. I also got the same sense of dread when thinking about future weekend or vacation plans. I was stressing even though I had nothing to stress about. This sense of dread would sometimes come with panic attacks again. Once I went to work or on the trip it would go away, nothing bad ever happened and I was fine. That is pretty much the definition of anxiety though I guess.

I realized that this was not just environmental, and that maybe I would have to stay on medication for the rest of my life. I was exhausted and could no longer fight the constant anxiety on my own. Maybe because I had finally been on medicine for a while when I was at my worst, I could not go back to like before even once I was better. I now knew that all those years I fought it without help, I did not have to. I did not want to be like so many family members I had seen struggle and suffer needlessly their entire life and I did not want to make things harder on those around me when I did not have to.

Before we went through this my husband and I were complete opposite on some things. This was good though and we balanced each other in those areas. After going through all of this we have balanced each other out even more. I feel even more relaxed and I feel like he is even more responsible, thoughtful and committed. I now joke if I wish I had been this much fun in high school and college because I would have had a lot more fun, but at least I stayed out of trouble. My main regrets in life are not things I have done, but the things I did not do when I could, or times that I did not stand up for myself or others.

I was so worried about what people thought and so worried about staying out of trouble that I didn't enjoy life the way I do now. Even though I did not ask for the separation from my husband, when I got it and was alone for the first time ever in my life, I learned a lot about myself. We had been together since we were teenagers, so I always had to somewhat answer to him or my parents.

During the separation, I usually had at least a day or two every week where Jay had Aubrie.

It was hard to adjust to not having that time alone anymore when my husband came back, which is part of the reason he did three times before he stayed for good. I did not actually date anyone else during the separation. The last thing I wanted to do was jump right back into something else when I finally had this freedom. I did have a couple guy friends that I was talking to long distance that I hoped I might get to date once the divorce went through. The idea of a long-distance relationship where I could still have some freedom was appealing to me now, and like I said before, I had an instant connection with one of those guys.

When Jay first left, I lost ten pounds in a week and a half and people noticed. When I started getting treated for my depression, I also started dressing nicer and taking better care of myself again. I was wearing dresses a lot and again people were noticing. I started getting my confidence back and people noticed that too. I would get honked at while pumping gas or while bending over to change Aubrie's diaper. It felt good to get that attention and my husband noticed all this too. We had filed for divorce and it would have been fast because it was uncontested. It was going to take about three or four months before the decree came in the mail though, because of courthouse hours being shorter due to the economy.

When my husband left the first two times I was devastated and begged him not to leave. The next time he left, or really before that, I honestly didn't care anymore or at least I thought I didn't. About a month or two before the decree was supposed to arrive, my husband wanted to stop it. I didn't at first. Although it had taken me a long time, I had finally gotten to a point where I was more than comfortable moving on. The thought of dating kind of excited me, because I never really had before him. The thought of keeping that freedom for a little while did too.

I ended up dating my husband instead and it wasn't long before he was back at home for good. I still can't really tell you why I so easily gave it another try when I didn't think I would. I think mainly because if the divorce had gone through, I was not sure if I could ever marry him again. Before we went through all we did I never thought about divorce as an option. Once he came back for good, I constantly thought about it any time things got hard. He had made it an option so now divorce was on the table.

It took me a long time to stop thinking about divorce every time things were hard, even though he was finally committed. He would tell me that if I was unhappy then for me to leave, because he was not again. When we committed to each other so young, everyone tried to warn us we might want to be date others more first. I think we both always wondered what it would be like dating more people, and that got easier to imagine the harder things got. What we came to realize was that we could move on with others and be okay, but we did not want to.

I know I will always struggle some with my OCD and Anxiety issues and like I said before, I may even be on medication for the rest of my life. Environmental stressors can make it worse though, whether I am on medication or not. The first time I changed jobs to get a less stressful one, it was one of the hardest decisions of my life. I was an HR Director in a retirement community. Doing that all day, and coming home to a baby and toddler, was very emotionally draining. At my job I had to fire and discipline people, listen to employee resident complaints and I got close to residents who would get worse physically and/or mentally or passed away. I feel the job did better prepare me in case I ever have to take care of parents or a spouse, but it was hard to give all I had to do that job all day, and then to my family as well when I got home.

I loved my old job and I enjoyed being in management, but it was so hard being a mom and a manager, while my husband was also a manager. It was also hard to sort of give up my career though. I had an office, a title and felt like in the long term, I would eventually make good money. I opted instead to take a little less money for a lot less stress. I could always try to get back into management later if I still wanted to.

Jay and I had taken turns throughout our marriage so far being the breadwinner. It was weird to let him stay in the lead for now, although relieving at the same time. I was the breadwinner when I got laid off from my job before that, which is another reason that was so hard. It was also hard because no matter the reason, when your employment ends, it can feel like a painful breakup, especially when the relationship lasts for years, and you feel like you gave your all to that company.

I am happier now with more work life balance. Even my husband eventually changed to a company that allows more work life balance, while also somehow earning more money. I will admit that makes me jealous. Every chance I have ever had to make more money was not much more money, and took me sacrificing my family and personal life, so it was just not worth it.

When I recently went through a lot of stress for the first time in years due to a change in bosses, I started noticing I was doing something most would not consider a sign of OCD and anxiety, but my doctor does. He says he realizes someone has it when they send him very long emails with run-on sentences and no paragraphs. Anyone who knows me wells know I have done this a lot in my life, not just in writing but in telling stories in person as well. My doctor jokingly wrote me a prescription to paragraph once. Once I learned this was a symptom, I now often write out emails or responses on Facebook without ever sending them. Journaling and writing this book helped me so much too for the same reason. It feels like you must get all your thoughts out of your head at that moment because it is overwhelming you. Or you think you will forget and never be able to say them again.

Chapter 7

I Couldn't Walk So I Had to Use Religion and Other Crutches

I was raised a Christian in the South. When I first started getting depressed, I questioned God for the first time and even yelled at him. I eventually turned back to church and religion to get through it though. I was not intentionally using it as a crutch. Some people say others use religion as a crutch. My doctor told me during this that he thinks it helps people get better sometimes but only because it moves the responsibility off them onto God. I explained to him that was not the case with me. I don't think you can just ask forgiveness and that is it and not feel guilty anymore. It is not quite that simple. It is and it isn't. It was a whole process for me of forgiving myself and asking for forgiveness from God, and others and truly changing. He then said that he was open-minded.

Even if you want to call religion a crutch, I still considered it a better crutch than certain other things like drugs or alcohol. Like I said before, at first, I didn't turn to my religion as a crutch but turned away from it instead. When I prayed and didn't feel like my prayers were being answered, I started to question whether God even existed. Even when I did believe in him, I was mad at him and felt further from him than ever before. The friends and family who treated me the worst during this time were also Christians so that turned me away as well, although some of the ones who treated me the best were also Christians.

I was only twelve years old when I got saved and hadn't done much wrong at all. When I went through my depression, it was the first time in my life I did a lot of things I would have to forgive myself for and ask forgiveness from God and other people for. It was the first true test of my religious beliefs. Did I really believe I could be forgiven? I also had a lot of awful stuff done to me by others while going through it. Could I really forgive them?

Before that, I had been with the same guy since I was sixteen years old. I had never even smoked a cigarette or been drunk. I did not drink until I was almost twenty-two because I was so scared of being like my alcoholic father. I finally realized I did not have his addictive nature except when it came to Dr. Pepper. I finally smoked a cigarette at twenty-nine to see what it was like just because I never had. I have since done it a few times socially, but not much because my husband cannot stand it.

I even started cursing some during this experience which weirded my husband out, even though he had cursed some for as long as I have known him. When we had just graduated high school and were on a senior trip with friends, I was trying to bleep out a curse word when singing, and accidentally bleeped out the wrong word. It was so shocking for me to curse, even to all my friends in the car that did, that the one driving almost ran off the road. On that same trip, since we had all turned eighteen recently, we all went to the back room of one of the stores at the beach for the first time. I was already so embarrassed even though we did not know anyone else. Next thing you know, I accidentally knocked down one penis water bottle which knocked all the penis water bottles in the place down. My face was so red. We all still laugh about that to this day.

While going through my PPD, I still didn't commit what most would consider major sins. I had thoughts that if I had acted on would have been, but I never acted on them. I still felt just as guilty as if I had. I also felt guilty for losing my temper with Aubrie, even though it was usually in the middle of the night when I was half asleep. I felt guilty because I tried to let her cry it out and she threw up once. I felt guilty because that made me mad at her, like she had some evil plan for me to never sleep again. I felt guilty because I did not just hold her whenever she wanted and let her sleep with me whenever she wanted. I felt guilty that I believed people when they said you could spoil a baby. Some will still swear by the cry out method and always making your kid stay in their own room and bed, but it just did not work for me and this kid. Whatever works for you and yours may be different.

Some people are okay once they get treated and start to get better with just saying that they had PPD, and now they are better. I still felt guilty for the way I had acted and things I had thought and done. I still felt the need to forgive myself and ask God and others for forgiveness. I wanted to do things to get back to my old self, or really an even better new version. I wanted to take better care of myself and not be so OCD. I wanted to be even happier and even more selfless and moral. As I said earlier, the political and religious beliefs I have now that I am fully recovered are different from the ones I had before I got depressed. I think them changing back and forth from one extreme to the other during my depression was also just part of me trying to figure them out. I also really needed unconditional love and support from my Sunday School class gave during that time and will be forever grateful for it.

I had always thought I was so selfless. Then I had a child. Then I later got two dogs. Before Aubrie we did not even have our own dog. We did as children but not as adults and the main caregivers. When I do something, I put everything I have into it and try to do it right. My first job was at a vet, so my dogs must have every shot, everything for fleas and heartworms, etc. because I have sat with dogs that died from not having it. I walk them as often as possible and try to take very good care of them. I am the same way with parenting. I want to do such a good job but being that selfless truly is hard and makes you realize how selfish you could be before.

I tried taking care of a puppy once in college. This other college student let me test her out for a couple days. I realized it was too much work for me at the time. I felt so guilty, but I did not realize how hard it would truly be. I even tried getting a dog amid recovering from my PPD. It was not planned but someone at work could not take care of this 8-month old puppy and what better to cheer me up than a puppy? We ended up just foster parenting her and finding her a better home.

At the time my husband and I were still off and on again and both working a lot. We did not have a fence or the time to dedicate to training this puppy that still was not house-trained and chewed everything. I did get her all her shots and even had her spayed and found her a wonderful forever home where she is spoiled and loved like crazy, even to this day. We even got to go visit her any time we wanted afterwards.

Before having a child or pets, I had a lot of free time. I got a lot of rest and took great care of myself. I also had a lot to give to my husband and job and others. None of this takes as much as you must give to someone you are the main caregiver for though. Caring for another human being or an animal that is totally dependent on you, is a lot of responsibility and you must give a lot to do it well. I had no idea, until I did both, what it truly took and what sacrifices I would have to make to do it as well as I wanted to. You are going to make mistakes, but I always joke, at least don't repeat your parents' and make your own new ones.

As I edit this book right now my daughter is almost 11 years old. She just received an award at school. She was the only one in her school to receive this. It was for having exemplary character. She is not just smart, more importantly she is kind and has great character. My husband and I also got an award recognizing us for our great parenting and it felt good. Parenting is hard but it gets easier with time and practice just like everything else.

Religion was not just a crutch I used. It has always been a big part of my life. I guess I used a lot of crutches to get better- church, prayer, pills, therapy, research, and exercise, just to name a few. I didn't use drugs, alcohol or anything else that would harm me or another person, so I am okay if other people want to call what I used crutches. I couldn't walk, I needed crutches.

When I asked my doctor whether he thought someone had to have pills or therapy to get better, his response was that a fire will eventually burn out if you don't put it out, but it usually does a lot more damage first. I probably needed more therapy than I went to, but it was so expensive. I also weaned off pills way too early as I mentioned before and eventually got on them again. They are even supposed to be safe to continue taking if I get pregnant again and if I breastfeed.

You cannot just have enough faith and try to be a good person and pray enough to get yourself out of depression. I tried that. It took me hitting an all-time low, which was my husband leaving me, for me or anyone else to even realize what was wrong with me. Even then I argued with my family at first that I was fine. I had just changed or finally realized who I really was, and they just didn't love me for me. I think the reason I was saying that though is because through this I did learn some things

94

about myself and I wanted to change for the better. You regress a lot though while trying to get better.

I like to joke that when I was going through PPD it was like on TV when you have that little angel on one shoulder and the little devil on the other. When you are going through any kind of depression, I think the little devil keeps yelling louder and louder until you can hardly hear the little angel anymore. Don't worry, I wasn't really seeing angels and devils, but I was having tons of random thoughts go through my head, I felt like I couldn't control. It felt like every day the positive ones got to be less and less while the negative ones increased.

I started getting better when I started listening to that little angel again and ignored the little devil. I started getting better again when I quit being angry at the angel voice and started to be angry at the devil one instead- the voice making me think I was a horrible wife, mother, person and that I had gone too far and lost my innocence and would never be the same, the one that made me want to give up. In the words of Billy Joel again, "Once I thought my innocence was gone. Now I know that happiness goes on."

Chapter 8

I Didn't Even Know the Cat Was in the Bag

The day we came home from the hospital, I had
hardly slept in two days. We got home which I thought
would be a relief but suddenly reality set in. We are home
with this baby, and no one is here to help us. There are no
nurses or family. I am not babysitting like in the past
waiting for her parents to come pick her up- this is real.
Suddenly, I was feeling overwhelmed. This is also the
point where hormones set in and crying and laughing at the
same time started.

About three years later, I talked to a friend who
confessed to me that she had PPD when her child was first
born. It was another case where I had no idea, but she told
me because I opened up about mine. Like me, she babysat a
lot and had always been around kids before having one.
When she had her son, it was like she kept waiting for the
parents to come pick him up, like she was babysitting.
Then she realized no was ever coming to get him, and she
wanted to just take him back to the hospital. She felt no
connection to him. I can totally relate to this.

Babysitting does not prepare you for parenthood. I
think it only prepares you for being a grandparent, where
you get to have fun with them, spoil them and give them
back. (I can't wait for that by the way.) Don't get me
wrong, babysitting is good practice but nothing like the real
deal. My friend never told anyone what she was feeling,
and eventually got over her PPD in a few months, and
started feeling connected to her child. She started working
out, lost a lot of weight, got a good job, and had some other

changes in her life that helped her adjust to parenthood. It was hard for her because her pregnancy was unplanned, and she was doing it with no spouse, but luckily had some help from family, which also helped her get back to feeling like her old self.

Another friend told me she almost drove into a pole with her daughter in the car years ago. She thought it would be okay because she was taking her with her. By the time she went to the doctor, her child was two and my friend was diagnosed with Anxiety. She had been suffering for a long time in silence and didn't bring up that story at the doctor's office. I realize now how women start rationalizing actions like this in their head as good for them and their child. When I was very depressed, I said that I felt guilty for bringing a child into this horrible world in front of my husband once, and I remember him looking at me like I was crazy.

I can't even say how many people have confessed their PPD to me since I opened up about my experience. I was just being open and honest and real like I always try to be. Some women treated me like a hero and others acted like I was revealing some secret I wasn't supposed to, although that wasn't the majority thankfully. I did not realize so many people went through this, and that there was still so much shame involved. The worst part about it is the people who treated you completely normal when you were keeping it inside and acting like you were okay but wishing you were dead, suddenly worried about you and constantly told you that you needed help once you opened up, and were actually getting help.

Everyone starts to feel bad they missed the signs before. They start to look for ones now. Even as you are getting better, everything you are doing is a sign you need more help, even though you are already getting all the help you possibly can, it just takes time to work. The fact that I was late all the time started to concern my mother, until I reminded her that I had always been late all the time. Everyone has their weaknesses. After having my pointed out so much during all of this I started to work on them more than ever before.

To this day I am working on being late, but it is still hard for me. I think it is the part of me that has always tried to fight against my OCD and be the opposite. For instance, when Aubrie was born, I was so worried about becoming one of those moms obsessed with schedules when it came to sleep, eating etc. that I think I went too far the other way. I was lucky that my mom was able to keep Aubrie and she never had to go to daycare but the only downside to this was no schedule.

We put Aubrie in preschool before Kindergarten because although she was prepared academically already, she was not prepared for the schedule. The longer she was on a schedule due to school, the better life got for all of us. To this day, she requires more sleep and an earlier bedtime than most children her age. All children are different but if I had known this earlier, I would have been a lot stricter with her schedule. This would have been a challenge for me though as I always have trouble not taking it to far one way or the other due to my obsessive compulsion.

I have read that people who are late are usually the most optimistic people. They are not trying to be rude, selfish, entitled or cause you any trouble. They believe they can fit more tasks into a short time than others do and thrive on multitasking. This is true for me, but it is also because I am trying to be more relaxed, and when you are constantly on a schedule that is impossible to do. I have so much trouble relaxing already. I am tense almost all the time. When I first went to my massage lady after getting on medication for my OCD and Anxiety, she was amazed that all the knots were gone. It may be time for me to try a new medication, because the knots and tension are back. I plan on discussing with my doctor soon.

When I was twenty-one years old, I fell down the stairs and caught myself, but slammed my left hand and butt into the ground hard. I quickly realized the heel on my shoe had broken, and that is why I had suddenly fallen. Well that, and because I was not holding on tightly to the rail as I do as I go downstairs now. It took me a moment to get up. As I hobbled to the car, I laughed as my husband and sister saw me and started laughing. They were picking me up that day to go to a family reunion after work. The shoe salesman also laughed when we had to stop by the store and buy me new shoes on the way. I was a little sore but okay and laughed about it with them. A year later, I started to get severe pain in my upper left arm, shoulder area. This would sometimes get worse and move into my neck and head as well. At its worst, I would describe the pain as comparable as or worse than giving birth with no epidural, except I did not get a baby each time, or a puppy-nothing.

That injury was sixteen years ago and as I write this now, I still have some occasional pain. I quickly realized the pain worsened when I was stressed, sick or on my period. It turned out to be a pinched nerve. Over the years, my pain has lessened due to physical therapy, chiropractic adjustments, massage, pain pills and over the counter pain relievers and nerve pain relievers, ice packs, cortisone injections, my OCD anxiety medication, yoga and other exercise, diet, reducing my stress and resting more. If I feel the pain come on, the faster I rest and do some of these other things to relieve the pain the faster is seems to go away. It does not get as severe now. I even regularly do some of these things, even when I am not hurting, to prevent the pain from coming back as bad or as often, including massage. I used to try to work through it or continue to care for my child, the house, etc. even while in agonizing pain which worsened my depression and anxiety.

While recovering, I found the most comfort in talking to others going through the same thing. The more I recovered the more I seemed to be able to help others. One person told me that her doctor didn't even understand her, but I did. I told her it is because I have been there. I told her if she keeps fighting, she will be okay. It does not feel like it now, and it makes you want to give up, but you will be okay as long you never stop fighting. She said she trusted me because I read her mind.

After recovering I had a girl at work come into my office. A while back I had given her a lot of baby clothes and shoes and stuff. She was having a baby girl and didn't have a lot of family to help her. I was cleaning out my attic and gave her enough to get her through until her daughter was about two years old. She said that because I had done this, she felt comfortable talking to me. She thought she had Postpartum Depression. She had come back to work only two weeks after having her baby due to financial reasons. She had no idea what I had been through, so I told her. I encouraged her to talk to her doctor and family, and she did, and got the help she needed. We became friends and checked on each often for a while after that.

At first, part of me was relieved to hear the same from others but part of me was angry. Why had they not shared this with me before? How did I not know that all these people around me had some of the same thoughts and were saying and doing some of the same things that I was so ashamed of? I have not only learned through all of this that the cat was in the bag, I learned why. It isn't as simple as no one talks about it because of shame. I realize now that some did not because they used to be ashamed or still were. Others just did not want to dwell on it because it was not a happy time in their life, and eventually you want to move on. I understand that more and more the longer it has been since I had it. However, I hope to never stop sharing completely.

All I wanted to hear when I was going through it was that I was not a monster; that others feel what I was feeling and I that it could get better. I felt so trapped like things would never get better. I took good care of my child, I still put her above everything, but I resented having to. Had I not had so much tragedy around me at the time I had my child, I think it would have been completely different for me. The truth is I think I could handle much more now. We always compare ourselves and each other to others, and others had been through worse than me, but at that point in my life that is the worst I personally had ever been through. I had a dream recently where I had a rash, but no one would help me because others around me had rashes that were worse. In the dream I was told to ignore it for this reason, but it kept itching and burning and getting worse.

The people who try to help you with tough love and being hard on you are shutting you out of their life mean well, but that is not what you need. At some points during you getting help, I think you need a little tough love thrown in there, for sure. I had some. More than anything, though, you need people to remind you that we all make mistakes and are human. We are here to support and encourage each other. You do learn going through this though who your real friends are. It is nice to know, as hard as it is to learn. Some people will completely shut you out of their life, because they don't have time to deal with your drama. Some people will take pity on you or help you in front of others but are never there when you truly need them. Some will judge you and guilt and shame you, but in the end, you see people's true colors and it is kind of relieving to know.

You get surprised by some who aren't there, but even more surprised by some of the ones who are. You see bad in some for the first time and good in others for the first time.

Even though we eventually ended up stopping it and working things out, I also had a divorce going on during this. Once the hard part was over, it was like I had a fresh start. It was hard because there were people in my life who I had once considered family, that I would not see much anymore and my relationship with them would forever change. I lost a lot of friends, or people I thought were friends. I had a new reputation, but I decided this could be a good thing. I was alone for the first time since I was sixteen years old. I had time to focus on things I never had before. I would even eventually have a fresh start at love. Also, since some people had this whole new idea of who I was, I didn't have all this pressure on me anymore to be this "perfect" person for some people.

It turns out some people who will drop you the moment they don't think you don't fit into their perceptions of how you should be, or the moment you are no longer in a place that it is convenient for them to hang out with you. Some people only want to hang out with you as a couple or a family, but as an individual or a single mother and her child, some no longer wanted to. It was a reality I had to face. Then there were the friends that were good friends, but they were also good friends to my ex-husband, so even if our friendship remained, it was going to change. Luckily, Jay and I worked things out, but having to face some of my worst fears ended up being a good thing in the long run. I wasn't scared of as much after all I went through.

The cat is also still in the bag because of misconceptions about Postpartum Depression. Everyone imagines what you see on the news which is mothers drowning their children in the bathtub or driving off bridges or into the ocean with their children in the car. You think this would scare everyone enough to make them want to stop people from getting to that point. Instead, people don't notice anything is wrong until it is almost that extreme, or even when it is not, they assume it is. Most cases of Postpartum Depression do not reach that point and that is usually Postpartum Psychosis which is a lot less common.

If you research, you will find different numbers but the most common I have seen is approximately 80% of women get "baby blues" the first two weeks within giving birth and get over this on their own. Between 10-20% develop Postpartum Depression, Anxiety and/or OCD which can occur up to a year after giving birth and can last for years if untreated. Postpartum Psychosis is even more dangerous but occurs in less than 1% of women, and because it is usually more obvious that they need help, most do not end up harming their baby or themselves.

What these numbers tell us is most women have feelings of depression after having a baby but that only a very small minority of women ever actually attempt to harm themselves or their children. Yet women are scared to be labeled with a postpartum mood disorder because people will think they might harm someone, and they might have their children taken away. It is a real fear. I had it.

I didn't even think of hurting my child, but I wished her away at times, and I prayed not to wake up at times. I thought if I told anyone what I was thinking they would take her away from me. It is ironic that one part of you is thinking that you don't want your child and the other part fears having them taken away. That was how it was for me. The truth is you just want help because you are feeling overwhelmed.

Chapter 9

Men Don't Get Depression and Women Don't Poot

     I have recently learned of two conspiracies. There are people who think men don't get depression, and people that think that women do not poot. Well, they either think that, or they just think that men shouldn't get depression and women shouldn't poot. My third, and probably more accurate theory, is that some people just don't think men should be open about having depression, and that women should not poot in front of other people. This way they can keep pretending that neither happens.

     You are probably wondering why I am going on so much about women pooting, so let me explain. Recently I was hanging out with a couple friends talking, when one of them stopped in the middle of the conversation. She said she had to walk outside for a minute and did, then came back in. This friend had been my friend for almost twenty years. She then explained that she had walked outside to poot because she has never done that in front of anyone before. When I started to think I could not recall ever seeing her doing that in the almost twenty years I had known her. I was thinking at that moment; she is one of these people behind the women don't poot conspiracy. I was already onto this for years before this for many reasons, but this moment, and a few others in the same year, really woke me up to how many people were in on this.

     My husband has always thought it was okay for men to do in front of others, but not women, and he acts like it is the most disgusting thing on earth if I ever do it. I have come across some men who were even raised not to do it in front of everyone. That is at least better than being raised that it is okay for men but not for women. My husband and I were jokingly arguing about this in the car one day with his mom riding in the backseat. She finally steps in and says, "Well I never did that in front of the boys growing up." Boy did that explain a lot. His mother was in on the conspiracy. I didn't have a chance in ever changing his mind about this.

I joke about a women not pooting conspiracy because it compares to another more serious one I feel goes on in the world, and that is that men don't get depression, especially not Postpartum Depression. Hormones played a role in my depression, but every woman deals with those same hormones when they have a baby. Why do some get depressed and others don't? A lot of depression is situational, and it happens to men too. I got depressed because of deaths and a layoff around the time I had a baby, and genetics, not just hormones.

Around ten percent of fathers are estimated to get Postpartum Depression. I think my husband got depressed. Will he ever admit it? He will admit he was affected by what I went through and anyone who knows him can tell you that, but I don't think he ever come out and truly say he had depression. Most men wouldn't. He was even more against pills and therapy than I was and would never try anything long enough for it to work. As I got better, he seemed to also. I almost felt like I was getting better for both of us at times.

When I would try to tell everyone there was something wrong with my husband when he left me, no one would believe me. Instead the reaction was concern about me embarrassing him by even implying there was. I was just concerned about him, but I had to quit worrying about it and just focus on getting better myself. It took me two years to get help and I think it took at least that long to completely recover.

One minute my husband would say we were over and that there was no hope we would ever work things out. The next he would say maybe we would get back together one day or if we ever wanted to, we could just go get remarried the next day like getting divorced was no big deal. He expected me to instantly get over the fact he was leaving me, and just be friends with him and okay with everything. Sure, I was going to be civil for Aubrie but nothing more. It crushed him when I said that other than the fact it gave me Aubrie, I regretted ever being with him at all. He related to broken heart songs in the same way I did even though he was the one leaving me. When we went to therapy and she asked us if we could find someone else what they would be like, he said he would find someone like me. Why would you leave someone to find someone else like them? It made no sense.

I said I would be with someone completely different. Why in the world would I knowingly put myself through this pain again? Why would I put myself through it the first place if I could go back in time? There is no other reason than for Aubrie to exist. That is how I felt at the time. Even now when we talk about it, he says he always saw us getting back together, even though that does not line up with his past actions and words. Of course, at the time his actions and words did not line up from day to day or minute to minute, which is why I was so confused and worried. I told him I could get through a divorce and I could get through the PPD but not both at the same time. He left anyways and I had to decide to get better with or without him.

Now I realize, as I wrote earlier in this book, I had already left my husband mentally and broke his heart without realizing it. After we later got back together for good, my husband developed an obsession with a band called the Avett Brothers. We went to see them in concert together and as I noticed him tearing up during one song, I realized why he related to and loved their music so much. The song was called Shame and here are enough lyrics for you to understand what I mean:

"Okay so I was wrong about, My reasons for us fallin' out, Of love, I want to fall back in, My life is different now I swear, I know now what it means to care, About somebody other than myself, I know the things I said to you, They were untender and untrue, I'd like to see those things undo, So if you could find it in your heart, To give a man a second start, I promise things won't end the same, Shame, boatloads of shame, Day after day, more of the same, Blame, please lift it off, Please take it off, please make it stop, Okay so I have read the mail, The stories people often tell, About us that we never knew, But their existence will float away, And just like every word they say, And we will hold hands as they fade…I felt so sure of everything, My love to you so well received, And I just strutted 'round your town, Knowing I didn't let you down, The truth be known, the truth be told, My heart was always fairly cold, Posing to be as warm as yours, My way of getting in your world, But now I'm out and I've had time, To look around and think, And sink into another world, That's filled with guilt and overwhelming, Shame…And everyone they have a heart, And when they break and fall apart, They need somebody's helping hand, I used to say just let 'em fall, It wouldn't bother me at all I couldn't help then, now I can."

During recovery and after, I joined an online support group on Facebook that included women all over the world. One day on this page someone posted a survey about Postpartum Depression with some of the most common symptoms listed. While going through it, I realized I had thirty of the thirty-two. I later realized I actually had all thirty-two.. I did not really ever think of myself as being scared to leave the house but I did have anxiety about leaving the house or doing pretty much anything at one point. I also did not self-harm or attempt suicide but I did have suicidal thoughts. I had all thirty-two and no one noticed I had it for two years. I didn't notice I had it for two years. The symptoms can look different in different people and it makes it hard to see sometimes. For instance, I know of women who had no bad feelings towards their child or about their child but did about everyone and everything else instead. A lot of times these women are so obsessed with keeping their child safe that they constantly worry about something happening to them. Even though I did have regrets about having Aubrie at times or jealousy towards her or wanted to run away etc. I still had this symptom.

I was so overprotective when it came to anything that could harm or kill her, such as swimming or getting into certain things around the house, etc. When it came to certain things she could eat or drink or her being on a schedule, I was as laid back as could be. Even on the playground, I did not hover. I was cautious but not obsessive about her getting hurt, but when it came to the life or death things, I was obsessively protective. This does not sound like such a bad thing, except when it consumes you and becomes dangerous for your mental health. I also feel like when I did this, I passed anxiety onto my child. For instance, she feared swimming for the longest time I feel due to this. With the next child I may do like I have seen others do, just throw a life jacket on them and keep an eye on them.

You can't see it when it is yourself and you don't talk to anyone about it because you are ashamed. You think you are just a bad person and that if you just snap out of it, and be a better person, or have more faith, it will go away. I waited for that to happen for two years and as I waited, I got more and more symptoms until I had all thirty-two. Awareness is so important.

As a society we need to start looking for these signs, not only in new mothers but in any woman or man who has a baby or toddler. In some women it even starts when they are pregnant, and it can go undetected for a long time. Society is still so misinformed about this and other mental illnesses. Most statistics you read will tell you that women get depression a lot more than men, which all that really means is women get help a lot more than men. It does not mean just as many men don't get it.

I don't remember getting a lot of information or any screening for depression or anxiety before or after having a baby, yet you do get screened for gestational diabetes while pregnant, even though it only affects 2.5% of women. Not that I am against screening for gestational diabetes, although all of us women do hate drinking that sugary drink,, but why would you screen for something that affects less than 3% and not screen for something estimated to affect up to 20%?

Here are the thirty-two symptoms of Postpartum Depression that were mentioned in the survey I saw. Some of these are also symptoms of Postpartum Anxiety or Postpartum OCD. I experienced all of these:

- angry outbursts
- anxiety/worry/panic
- appetite changes
- attachment or connection to my baby missing

- concentration/lack of focus/forgetful
- loss of confidence/unsure of myself
- crying/sad/depressed/teary
- feeling like a failure/inadequate mother
- guilt and shame
- hopelessness/things will never improve
- despair/loss of power/helpless
- indecisive/changing my mind/confused
- irritability/agitation/cranky
- isolation/loneliness
- lack of joy
- loss of control/out of control
- loss of motivation and energy/enthusiasm
- negative/irrational thoughts
- not caring/numbness
- obsessive behaviors/manic about cleaning
- overwhelmed
- resentful of husband
- scared to leave the house
- self-loathing/hating self/critical of self
- self-harm, suicidal thoughts or attempts
- lowered self-esteem
- sleeping problems/insomnia
- stressed/unable to relax
- tired/exhausted/fatigue
- unable to cope/complete tasks
- unable to socialize/withdrawn from family and friends
- want to run away/don't want to be a mother

Chapter 10

Conversations with My Three-Year Old

I loved the age of three! My child was now
potty-trained, she talked in a way we could understand her
better, she understood us better, and we could take her out
places without wondering which child we were going to
get. Before she was three, even if she was well-fed,
well-rested and had a clean diaper, she may not by the time
you were in the middle of dinner or grocery shopping. She
might just get in a bad mood for any other reason on earth
too-her teeth hurt, she didn't get something she wanted or
for no good reason at all sometimes it seemed. You also
must love when they are potty-training and must go to the
bathroom five times during dinner. Once we got through
that stage it felt like I had a little comedian around all the
time. She cracked me up!

In one attempt to get out of bed, because she would
do anything to get out of bed, started with "But God said
you need to let me watch another movie." One night she
came into my room after being tucked in and said,
"Mommy, I just wanted to tell you that I love you so
much!" My response was, "I love you so much too baby,
but get back in the bed." When it came to bedtime, she
pulled out all the stops. At one point, if I didn't respond
fast enough to Mommy she started calling, "Amanda,
Amanda!" I responded to this one night to find her so
excited about something she had found she wanted to hand
to me. I reached out and grabbed it and then she said,
"Here Mommy, this is a booger, I got out of my nose all by
myself with my finger!" I couldn't help but just burst out
laughing and think, "Ah, the joys of motherhood."

One day she started to drag our foot massager out of the closet, and we told her that it was not a toy and she needed to put it back and her response: "but my feet hurt". Well, how do you argue with that? So, my husband massaged her feet while I plugged it in for her and then helped her use it. She later got in trouble for trying to unplug it herself. Her argument this time was that she didn't touch the part she wasn't supposed to. She proceeded to point at the part she wasn't supposed to touch. My husband still had a pretty long conversation with her about asking adults for help with certain things and things children are not supposed to do. Of course, that was after he paused for a moment and looked at me with a smile and that thought of, "How do you argue with a three-year old who is coming back with rational arguments?"

Most people think their child is a genius, but our three-year old could put together 64-piece puzzles alone and could almost do 100. She could do 24 pieces at age two and could write her name by then also. She they started working on her last name at age three, which I even spelled wrong for the first year Jay and I dated. At age two, she knew all her shapes, including hexagon and octagon, all her colors, numbers and letters. I have always loved school while my husband did not despite having a lot of book smarts himself. My husband has always loved learning on his own though. He reads History books bigger than the Bible and watches History and Science shows all the time. He also has a lot of common sense, which I lack. Combined this made our little genius daughter.

More importantly she is loved. Everywhere we go people say they can tell that she is a loved child because she is so happy and loving most of the time. My husband always jokes that no matter how hard we try we can't seem to screw her up. Even after all we have been through she could tell still we loved her and loved each other. We somehow showed it even in the worst of times. Even when we went to therapy our therapist said there was something special about us.

I always tell people though that when I call my child smart, it is not to brag. It is to say that it makes it very hard to have a child who is constantly trying to outsmart you and can. It is also a fun challenge and entertaining too though to say the least. Even though she is smart, she is also a social butterfly, she is beautiful, and like I said before, a little comedian. My mom asked Aubrie one day where she got all those mosquito bites from and she said, "From a mosquito". Another day, my husband asked her how to say open in Spanish because she knows how to from Dora and she said, "With your mouth". At that moment I realized that my husband must have born a smart aleck, because she already was one just like him.

She even manages to entertain in her sleep. Aubrie was so scared of the storms one night that we let her sleep with us. She talks in her sleep. Things I heard her yell out during the night included, "I don't want to do it, you do it!", "I want sausage. Go cook me some sausage!", and "I want ice cream!". She apparently also gets hungry in her sleep. I also love feeling like a child again with her in certain moments, like when we accidentally let a horse balloon, I had gotten her from my work go. It was one of the funniest things I've ever watched seeing it fly to horsy heaven. It looked like a horse really was flying. Luckily, we had another one. She ended up naming her Sally, which she names everything lately because I call her silly Sally. I may end up with a granddaughter named Sally, and if she has a boy, she is apparently going to name him Cocoa. We kept that other horse for weeks until she finally deflated.

I love curling up and watching cartoons with Aubrie, especially the ones I used to watch growing up. I love going to the park and playing with her, and could not wait to take her to the fair starting at age three! We also loved going to the pool and the water park. During a tornado outbreak, Aubrie asked if we could turn the weather channel off because it is not her fave-fave. When I took her to a jewelry store for the first time it was like she was at the candy store. She picked out a $2,000 ring and I told her she needed a fiancé first. She said that she didn't want the fiancé she just wanted the ring. I couldn't argue with that, but she did need a job first at least.

She wanted to come to work with me one day, so my mom brought her to have lunch with me. We went to Waffle House and when the waitress brought us our drinks Aubrie said, "Thanks, but where's our food?' She also asked if they had Wheels on the Bus on the jukebox. There were still some challenges at this age though. One day I stepped in a wet spot on the living room and asked Aubrie if she spilled some of her milk and her response was, "No mommy, that is peepee." Having a recently potty-trained child means the occasional accident and you sometimes feel like you have a puppy instead. However, for those of you still in the diapers and no sleep stage, it does get easier and you will miss the moments they wanted to be held a lot and sometimes you will miss the moments when they couldn't talk. You spend all that time wishing they could walk and talk and then they never stop doing either. I never thought I would have a child that talks more than I do.

You are constantly chasing them and being talked to but for the most part it is a blast once you get through the stage where they go after everything that could possibly hurt them. If only someone told you this line from the movie *The Change Up*, before you had kids, you might feel you were better prepared for parenthood: "Having children, it's like...living with little mini drug addicts. "Ya know, they're laughing one minute, and then they're crying the next, then they're trying to kill themselves in your bathroom for no good reason. They're very mean and selfish; they burn through your money..."

Chapter 11

Can I Have a Do-Over Please?

After going through all I did, I did not think I
wanted any more children at one point. People constantly
asked when Aubrie was younger. This was especially hard
when I was depressed and when my marriage was not so
good. It was harder years later when I could not get
pregnant and people did not know. So many close to me
still do not realize how traumatic having my first child was
for me. When someone else was talking about their
near-death experience having their child and how they did
not want another, I shared I used to not either, but I
eventually changed my mind. Someone else close to me
said, "But she went through a very traumatic experience".
        I get that I did not almost die giving birth and
neither did Aubrie. However, I got to the point I did not
even want to live anymore, and my marriage almost ended.
By the way, that other mother has since had another child
and it went a lot better for both this time luckily. I know
that person close to me did not mean any harm by what
they said but it still stung a little. It reminded me that my
mental anguish would never get the same sympathy
physical anguish does, even though it was worse for me
than any physical pain I have ever been through.
        A couple years after working things out, my
husband and I did want more children. He wanted more
before I did. When I asked him why and he said because
Aubrie was so awesome, he wanted more. How could I
argue with that great reason? It was a tough decision for
me but as I got older and realized I was running out of time,
I wanted them too. Years later we still only have one child,

mainly due to me having low progesterone. We still have some time and if it never happens, we may consider adoption. I would like to adopt anyways but I am still trying to sell my husband on it. I am very close with my stepfather who raised me even though we are not blood. That and the fact that there are so many children without homes have both given me the desire to adopt.

I want a do-over, even though I will never really get one. Not with Aubrie, not really. I can't do her babyhood over again. All I can do is to love her as much as possible now and in the future and try to make up for it. As I write this today, she is now almost eleven and is probably one of my best friends, along with Jay and my parents. Some people don't think you should be friends with your child, but I disagree. If you can still discipline them when needed I think it is great to be so close with them. I hope we stay as close as she ages and that our relationship continues to progress as we age.

I am closer to my mom now that we are both older than I was at a younger age. I relate to her more now than ever. I have always been close to her and my stepdad but was probably more of a Daddy's girl at a younger age. I still turn to my dad for many things including car trouble, financial advice and dead mice in the washer of course. When Jay and I went through all we did though, my Dad was angry at Jay and it was easier to talk to my mom about it. Jay had worked for her in the past and she grew close to him during that time so she stayed as neutral as she could.

I would like another shot at babyhood with another child. I think I could handle it much better after all I have learned. I finally get excited to see babies and baby stuff again which is nice to feel again. In a weird career twist, after leaving that job with the bad boss I now work at a daycare and love it. I am now around kids all day the ages Aubrie was when I went through my depression. I enjoy this because I feel like I am getting to enjoy some things about her age I missed out on and it helps with the baby fever for now. I am losing weight and getting healthier doing it instead of an office job, which might also help in my attempt to get pregnant. I also feel like I am almost conquering a fear or proving something every day probably more to myself than anyone else. It was never about me being a bad mom, or bad with children or not liking children. I love and adore children. I always have and I still do. I don't really fear getting PPD again. Even if I did get it again, I know everyone would realize much sooner this time and I would get the help I need. I was hoping I would have more kids by now and could write that I did not get it again or that is was handled better caught earlier, etc. I can tell you I know of women this has been the case with though.

If I have learned anything in life it is that you really don't get a do-over, but you do get a second chance. I kept trying to get back to the same person I was before but that was not possible. I was different but I finally realized that was not a bad thing. If I ever went through the same thing again, I would be more prepared, I was stronger. Even if I never went through the same again, I know I will go through hard times. That is just a part of life. Now I feel better prepared for this though. People say time heals and it does, but you are forever scarred. Most of the time, it is hard for me to remember feeling as badly as I did. Occasionally, something, often a song will remind me, and I will remember that pain just for that moment.

There are people I have not been able to make peace with, some I mentioned before. This bothers me so much. I am such a sensitive person and any relationship I have had end with a person in a bad way always sits with me forever. As time goes on, I have gotten better at dealing with it though. I finally realize I cannot control their reaction and can only control mine. I cannot force them to hear me or understand me or to like me or to care. I also sometimes realize some people are just not the kind of people I want in my life. Some do not accept me for me, some do not treat you and/or others very well and sometimes people just get so passionate about certain beliefs that they put those above loving others. Some are also not in a good place mentally themselves and you try to be close to them anyways, but sometimes it is not worth the toll on your own mental health. Despite all of this, that moment you realize you are never going to have a deeper connection or closer relationship with someone when you want to and have tried can be so painful.

If Jay had never left, I think I would have gotten better without getting as bad as I did and without getting as much help as I eventually needed. However, I might have not gotten the help I needed for my general OCD and Anxiety like I did. Also, like a lot of other women, I am not sure I would have ever completely realized I had Postpartum OCD/Anxiety/Depression. After sharing my story, I have had many women tell me they think they had it long ago without realizing. I think I was starting to get better right before Jay left and was starting to realize something was wrong.

I remember watching one of my favorite shows at the time *One Tree Hill*. I was watching an episode where one of the main characters was depressed because her mom had died. At one point she accidentally knocked over a candle and the piano caught fire and she did not even seem to notice or care. She just sat there in a daze. Her husband eventually moved her out of the way. In another part, she went and jumped into their pool and floated to the bottom and stayed there. Her husband once again jumped in and saved her, not understanding what she was doing. I don't think she was trying to kill herself. I think she just wanted

119

someone to save her or she just did not care one way or another. I sadly related completely to her. I knew exactly how she felt, and I knew this meant something either had been or was wrong with me and that this was not normal.

I recently saw a quote that said, "Even though your wounds are not your fault, your healing is still your responsibility." This took me a long time to realize myself. Most of the time you don't get rescued and even if someone tries to, they often fail despite their best efforts. You must want to get better yourself and you must fight and save yourself most of the time. I never thought I would relate to people who did not want to live anymore. I used to get angry at people who died by suicide. Like a lot of people, I thought it was selfish. I now know that the people who get to that point do not mean to be selfish at all and I have more sympathy and less judgment. They don't realize they are just passing the pain onto others who love them. They truly believe you will be better off without them and they are suffering so badly and just want to make it stop. There are better ways to make it stop.

I never tried to kill myself or planned it out, but I did want to die at times. I am not sure if there had not been a pill in front of me, I could have easily taken that I would not have at certain points. I am glad I did not though. Life is better than ever for me now and I hope to make others realize it can be for them too.

Helpful Links and Resources

If you believe you may have postpartum OCD, Anxiety, depression or any other mood disorders, please talk to your doctor. I also encourage you to try and find a support group. If you do not feel comfortable going to one in person there are many confidential ones available online including Facebook. You can talk to people all over the world that are currently experiencing the same thing or have in the past. There are also a lot of online websites and resources that may be useful to you. Here are some links I found helpful below. Some are simply parenting or motivational sites, but they also made me not feel alone as a parent and some even helped me find humor in even the worst parts of parenting,

If you think someone you know might have it, please give them this book to read, encourage them to talk to their doctor, find a support group and/or to use the resources below:

Websites:

www.postpartumprogress.com

https://www.postpartum.net/

www.jennyslight.org

www.postpartummen.com

www.healthyplace.com

www.scarymommy.com

www.babycenter.com

www.lindahenley-smith.com

https://www.facebook.com/lifeofdad/

Made in the USA
Coppell, TX
18 May 2021